Employment Issues in the European Union

Internationale Marktwirtschaft

Herausgegeben von
Gustav Dieckheuer, Karl-Hans Hartwig und Theresia Theurl

Band 6

PETER LANG
Frankfurt am Main · Berlin · Bern · Bruxelles · New York · Oxford · Wien

Gustav Dieckheuer/Bogusław Fiedor (eds.)

Employment Issues in the European Union

PETER LANG
Europäischer Verlag der Wissenschaften

Bibliographic Information published by Die Deutsche Bibliothek
Die Deutsche Bibliothek lists this publication in the Deutsche Nationalbibliografie; detailed bibliographic data is available in the internet at <http://dnb.ddb.de>.

ISSN 1615-939X
ISBN 3-631-55439-7
US-ISBN 0-8204-9937-4

Printed in Germany 1 2 3 4 6 7

www.peterlang.de

Introduction

Nowadays persistent unemployment is one of the main economic problems in Germany as well as in other countries of the European Union. For many years economic growth has obviously been too low to give impulses strong enough to improve the situation on the European labour markets effectively. There are several reasons for this situation: keen competition on markets for tradable goods, structural changes in the globalization process, labour market regulations, sticky wages for low qualified workers, missing incentives for lifetime learning, transformation frictions in the new EU-countries.

These topics compose the background of a collection of articles published in this book. The articles mainly deal with the following aspects: causes of unemployment in the European Union, technological changes, skills and structural unemployment, institutional conditions on labour markets, importance of international trade and foreign direct investment, employment effects of monetary policy, chances and risks of liberalized labour markets.

The papers were presented at a German-Polish conference held at the University of Münster in 2005. Due to the universities participating in the conference (Wrocław University of Economics, Poland, and University of Münster, Germany) the problems in several papers are aimed at the European Union, focussing on a special country's perspective, precisely Germany and Poland.

The institutional frame of this conference is a co-operation between Wrocław University of Economics (former Oskar-Lange-Academy) and the Faculty of Economics at the University of Münster which started in 1971 – at a time when social systems and economic thinking were extremely different in East and West. Since then every two years conferences have been held on many different themes, e.g. institutional aspects of market and planned economies, price theory and policy in different economic systems, theory and policy of income distribution, chances and risks of international openness, political management of the transition process, direct investment as a factor of economic development, sustainable economic development, environment and trade in a globalized economy, as well as the eastward enlargement of the European Union.

This co¬operation was dominantly initiated by Professor Dr. Dr. h. c. Jochen Schumann (University of Münster). He has promoted and partly organised the conferences as well as supported research work and exchange of ideas on an individual level for more than 25 years. Due to many economic problems, which are unsolved in both countries the co-operation will continue and conferences on other topics in currently important theoretical and political fields will follow.

Preparing the conference papers for publication required many activities of cross-border co-ordination as well as translation and formatting. These activities have mainly been conducted and supported by Julia Hornke, René Löffler and Marcel Mlakar at the University of Münster. We would like to express our gratitude to them.

Münster, March 2006.

Gustav Dieckheuer and Bogusław Fiedor

Contents

Unemployment and Poland's Monetary Policy in the Years 2003-2004 9
Stefan Linek and Marian Noga

Can Polish Monetary Policy Contribute to Mitigating the Unemployment Problem? 17
Maria Piotrowska

Is investing abroad unpatriotic? Jobs and investment in an expanding EU 29
Aloys Prinz

Skill-biased technical change and structural unemployment in Europe 45
Thomas Apolte

International trade and employment: A sectoral and regional analysis for Germany and the EU25 59
Gustav Dieckheuer

Benchmarking International Employment and Growth Performance: The Bertelsmann Foundation Approach 83
Ulrich van Suntum

Foreign Direct Investment and the Labour Market in Poland 93
Jan Rymarczyk and Jerzy Rymarczyk

The Labour Market in the Polish-German Cross-border Area: Institutional Aspects 107
Franciszek Adamczuk and Andrzej Graczyk

The Institutional Aspects of Personal Capital Investments 119
Bożena Klimczak

Uncertainty and Risk in Perfectly Flexible Labour Market 129
Bogusław Fiedor and Andrzej Matysiak

Unemployment and Poland's Monetary Policy in the Years 2003-2004

by

Stefan Linek and Marian Noga

1 Introduction

In the countries of Eastern and Central Europe – also including Poland – the central planning economy has left a large hidden unemployment, which has risen to the surface during the transformation process. The problem of unemployment in the market economy has a rich literature on the subject; however, guidelines provided in this literature with respect to the factors decreasing unemployment cannot be readily applied to the Polish economy.

The purpose of this paper is not the analysis of the phenomenon of unemployment in Poland but the influence of unemployment on the formation of monetary policy in Poland. It is of interest inasmuch as monetary authorities in Poland are strictly assigned tasks by the constitution and other legal acts. The National Bank of Poland (the NBP) as the central bank of the State – according to the constitution – "shall be responsible for the value of Polish currency". However, the act on the NBP of 1997 in article 3 determines that "the basic objective of the NBP shall be to maintain price stability, and it shall at the same time act in support of Government economic policies, insofar as this does not constrain pursuit of the basic objective of the NBP". The above-defined objective of monetary authorities signifies such actions that inflation should be as low as not to exert negative influence on investments, savings and other important decisions made by participants in economic life. What relationships can be determined between unemployment and monetary policy? In the literature on the subject one usually indicates the following relationships:

- First of all, it is the relationship between unemployment and inflation, expressed as the classical Phillips curve, or in Phelps-Friedman's version, or in the formulation of the theory of rational expectations;
- Second, it is the formulation of monetary policy as an instrument counteracting an economic recession, that is monetary policy as anticyclical policy and hence affecting a decrease in unemployment ;
- Third, monetarism proves by means of the AD-AS model that state monetary policy can be the cause of micro-cycles of economic conditions and thus increase or decrease unemployment. Hence monetarism introduces one of its main theses that economic policy is ineffective.

The authors of the present paper put forward the following working hypothesis: **in the period under examination of 2003-2004, Poland's monetary policy**

would have been decidedly more restrictive, if the unemployment rate in this period had been decidedly lower. At this point it is worth stressing that such an attitude toward monetary policy in the years of 2003-2004 in Poland was also affected by the very slowly growing total wage fund as well as a very high rate of productivity growth (10-15% on an annual scale). Proving this working hypothesis is of great significance because in Poland, monetary authorities are being criticized for not taking into consideration in their decisions problems of economic growth. So, if the working hypothesis of the paper is proven, the criticism of monetary policy in Poland during 2003-2004 from the point of view of its influence on economic growth should be considered pointless.

The proving of the working hypothesis will be conducted in the following sequence:

- First, we will show what the unemployment trends were like in Poland in the years 2003-2004;
- Second, we will show how Poland's monetary policy for the years 2003-2004 is constructed;
- Third, in conclusion we will present a simulation of how the monetary policy of this period would have been shaped if the unemployment rate had been much lower.

2 Unemployment trends in Poland in the years 2003-2004

The central planning economy has left a high hidden unemployment in Poland. The transformation period has revealed unemployment. In Table 1, we present the unemployment rate in Poland and in selected countries of Central and Eastern Europe.

Table 1: Unemployment rate (in %)

	II 2003	**III 2003**	**IV 2003**	**I 2004**	**02 2004**	**03 2004**	**04 2004**	**05 2004**	**12 2004**
Poland	**19.9**	**19.5**	**19.6**	**20.6**	**20.6**	**20.5**	**20.0**	**19.6**	**18.9**
Czech Republic	9.5	10.0	10.0	10.8	10.9	10.7	10.2	9.9	•
Slovakia	15.5	14.2	14.5	16.4	16.5	16.0	15.3	14.5	•
Slovenia	10.9	11.2	11.1	11.3	11.2	11.1	10.7	•	•
Hungary	6.0	5.7	5.5	6.0	6.0	6.1	6.0	•	•
Estonia	5.5	4.9	4.9	5.1	5.1	5.2	5.0	4.8	
Lithuania	10.1	9.5	9.6	8.0	8.1	7.9	7.5	7.0	•
Latvia	8.7	8.5	8.5	9.0	9.0	9.2	9.0	8.7	•
Bulgaria	14.3	13.0	13.2	14.1	14.2	13.7	13.2	•	•
Romania	7.4	6.7	7.1-	7.7	7.7	7.7	7.3	6.8	•

Source: National Statistical offices. The NBP.

From the data contained in Table 1, it follows that the unemployment rate in Poland in the years 2003-2004 was the highest rate among all the countries selected for the research.

In economic theory, scientific inquiries of the neoclassical and the Keynesian school treat the role of the state in the labour market in different ways. According to the neoclassical school, in free market economy conditions there occurs a tendency in the labour market to establish equilibrium between labour supply and labour demand, which is labelled as a state of full employment. If there appeared a surplus of labour supply in the labour market, then, according to neoclassical economists, competition between employees would cause a decrease in real wages; at lower wages, an increase in labour demand and a decrease in labour supply would ensue till the establishment of equilibrium at full employment, and any possible unemployment would then be voluntary unemployment resulting from lack of the acceptance of the offered wage rate. The introducing of various regulations by the state such as, for example, establishing a minimum wage or implementing unemployment benefits limits – according to neoclassical economists – natural market mechanisms. In the above-mentioned examples, this means the decreasing of wage flexibility from the bottom in the first instance and the reducing of competition on the supply side of the labour market in the second instance. Thus, according to neoclassical economists, every intervention in the labour market is undesirable.

Keynesian advocates view the issue of the labour market in a different way: they think that the normal state of economy is a state of disequilibrium characterized by insufficient demand for commodities; however, the state of economic equilibrium is an ideal state, that all aim to achieve. That is why, when there is not enough commodity demand to purchase the whole generated output, entrepreneurs are forced to decrease output, and consequently labour demand necessary to generate it. As a result of this, there occurs unemployment which is of a quite permanent nature and cannot be eradicated by means of automatic market mechanisms. Thus, according to Keynesian advocates, there is a need for active state intervention in economic processes in order to reduce unemployment.

The extent of labour market regulation in different member states of the European Union varies considerably, which is shown by means of values of the measure invented by the OCED (Table 2).

This measure takes into account:

1. individual standards of employment relationship protection
2. additional collective dismissal regulations
3. state solutions concerning part-time employment

The synthetic index is a weighted arithmetic mean of specific rates.

Table 2: Extent of labour market regulation in the states of the European Union and in Poland

Country	Individual Employment Protection	Additional collective dismissal Regulations	Part-time Employment Regulations	Synthetic Index
Great Britain	0.8	2.9	0.3	0.9
Ireland	1.6	2.1	0.3	1.1
Denmark	1.6	3.1	0.9	1.5
Finland	2.1	2.4	1.9	2.1
Holland	3.1	2.8	1.2	2.2
Austria	2.6	3.3	1.8	2.3
Belgium	1.5	4.1	2.8	2.5
Sweden	2.8	4.5	1.6	2.6
Germany	2.8	3.1	2.3	2.6
France	2.3	2.1	3.6	2.8
Spain	2.6	3.1	3.5	3.1
Italy	2.8	4.1	3.8	3.4
Greece	2.4	3.3	4.8	3.5
Portugal	4.3	3.6	3.0	3.7
Poland	**2.2**	**3.9**	**1.0**	**2.0**

Source: OECD Employment Outlook, 1999, taken from Wiśniewski 2003, page 56.

The data contained in Table 2 leads, first of all, to two conclusions:

- First, we have to do with the weakest domestic labour market regulation in Great Britain and Ireland, thus in the countries where the economy is traditionally based on neo-liberal economic thought.
- Second, the extent of labour market regulation in Poland in comparison with the countries of the "old" European Union is relatively low. This, first of all, follows from low levels of part-time employment regulation; however, the extent of collective dismissal regulation is relatively high.

Labour market deregulation – according to followers of this concept – is supposed to improve labour force allocation in the labour market. Economic growth occurs in Poland practically without creating jobs. According to various researches, employment in Poland will rise, when the dynamics of GDP on an annual scale surpasses 5%. This value is very high and much higher than in the USA (0.5%) and in the Europeans Union (2.8%). In the year 2004 the growth rate of GDP surpassed 5% and only now, practically after 3 years, did we observe a decrease in the unemployment rate and an increase in employment. Increasing employment in Poland will be possible, when, apart from maintaining the growth rate of GDP at a level of 5%, the labour market policy formula changes from a discouraging formula to a stimulating one. In Poland only a little more than 50% of people of productive age work; however, in highly-developed countries, this percentage amounts to 70%.

One of the main factors limiting prospects for increasing employment is a very high tax wedge, that is, the relationship between the tax burden and social charge contributions at one level and gross remuneration at another level. In the year 2002 this indicator amounted to 41.4% (for a single person obtaining 67% of the average remuneration in the national economy) and was higher than the average tax wedge in the European Union and in the countries joining the EU. The burdening of remuneration to such an extent is inevitable because the funds thus obtained must finance very big social transfer expenses – resulting mainly from a very large and still growing number of people obtaining retirement and disability pensions (vide Table 3).

Table 3: Tax wedge in the year 2002

Country	**Tax**	**Country**	**Tax**
Belgium	48.9	UE15	37.8
Germany	45.9	France	37.8
Sweden	45.9	Estonia	37.4
Romania	43.5	Holland	37.2
Italy	42.7	Bulgaria	35.5
Hungary	42.0	Greece	34.3
The Czech Republic	41.8	Spain	33.9
Latvia	41.4	Norway	33.8
Poland	**41.4**	Portugal	29.5
Lithuania	41.3	The USA	27.3
Countries joining the EU	41.1	Luxembourg	27.3
Denmark	40.4	Great Britain	24.7
Finland	40.4	Japan	23.2
Slovakia	40.3	Malta	18.1
Austria	39.9	Cyprus	17.5
Slovenia	39.9	Ireland	16.6

Source: Eurostat.

3 Guidelines and performance of monetary policy in Poland in 2003-2004

As it has been stressed in the introduction, the main objective of monetary authorities is to maintain stable price levels. In practice, this generally formulated basic objective of the activity of monetary authorities requires to be concretized. First, contemporary central banks understand price stability to mean the inflation rate at such low levels that it should not exert any negative influence on investments, savings, and other important decisions made by participants in economic life. Maintaining the so-defined price stability is the basic way that the central bank contributes with its decisions towards attaining high and constant economic growth. Second, apart from qualitatively determining the basic objective, assigning a certain numerical value to it is becoming a more and more common practice among central banks. This follows from the fact that in recent years more and more central banks are employing monetary policy in the framework of the so-called strategy of direct inflation target (DIT). Poland's monetary authorities in January 2003 determined the DIT at a level of 2.5% within a symmetrical band of permitted fluctuations of +/- 1 percentage point. In January 2004 the current Monetary Policy Council (MPC) confirmed the MPC's 2003 decision. The new MPC also expressed the opinion that Poland would profit the most from the adoption of an economic strategy oriented towards creating conditions ensuring the introduction of the euro in the shortest possible period of time.

The monetary policy instruments employed by the Monetary Policy Council are:

1. interests rates
2. open market operations
3. required reserves
4. credit and deposit operations
5. technical credit

Interest rates are a key instrument of carrying out the objective of the monetary policy that is being implemented. In the years 2003-2004 these interest rates were:

- reference rate
- lombard rate
- deposit rate
- rediscount rate

The reference rate determines the minimal profitability of money bills being sold within open market operations. Starting from the first of January 2003 till the end of the year 2004, the maturity of basic open market operations in the from of the emission of NBP bills was shortened from 28 to 14 days. The reference rate determines the current direction of monetary policy, at the same time affecting the interest rate for inter-bank deposits with similar maturities. From the first of January 2005, the maturity of NBP bills was shortened to 7 days.

The lombard rate determines the maximum cost of obtaining funds from the central bank for one day by the banks.

The deposit rate determines the price for making a one-day deposit in the NBP offered by the central bank.

The rediscount rate defines the cost of obtaining funds against bills of exchange from the central bank on an annual scale.

The lombard and deposit rates form the upper and lower ends of the corridor of central bank reference rate fluctuations. In the year 2003 the inflation rate was maintained below the DIT; as a result of this, the MPC lowered interest rates six times. The reference rate was reduced altogether from 6.75% to 5.25%, the lombard rate from 8.75% to 6.7%, the deposit rate from 4.5% to 3.75% and the rediscount rate from 7.5% to 5.75%. In effect, the corridor of interest rate fluctuations was narrowed down from 4.0 to 3.0 percentage points.

In the year 2004 as a result of a shock caused by joining the European Union, the MPC, in order to prevent a price spiral from occurring increased all interest rates three times, altogether by 1.25 percentage points. In such a way the NBP reference rate was formed at a level of 6.5% within a corridor of permitted fluctuations of 1.5 percentage points.

To help people communicate with monetary authorities, the MPC have introduced, besides the neutral approach to monetary policy (policy bias), the restrictive and the soft approach. The approach to monetary policy indicates the probable direction of future changes in interest rates.

The **restrictive** approach will mean that increasing NBP interest rates is more probable than lowering them. The **soft** approach will signal a higher probability of lowering interest rates rather than increasing them. The **neutral** approach will mean approximate probabilities of increasing as well as decreasing interest rates.

In the year 2003 the former MPC took only the neutral position in monetary policy. The current MPC announced the possibility of adopting one of the tree positions and in March 2004 the MPC adopted the restrictive position in monetary policy. This was closely connected with the remaining of the inflation rate above the DIT and with the inflation projection to the year 2006 all the time indicating a high probability that the inflation rate will remain above the DIT.

4 Conclusion

Could the decisions made by Poland's monetary authorities in the years 2003-2004 have been different? It seems that they could have, especially in the year 2004. Namely, the scale of increases in interest rates would have been larger, if the unemployment rate in Poland had been lower at that time. The objective of monetary authorities is to bring the existing inflation rate down to the level of direct inflation target. The basic instruments carrying out this objective are interest rates. An increase in prices entails pressure to increase wages, which in the literature on the subject is labelled as a price and wage spiral. The existing high unemployment rate in Poland has impeded pressure to increase wages because this threatens to create job losses. In this situation the total wage fund is increasing very slowly, slower than work productivity. In this situation the monetary policy of the state is becoming less restrictive and thus the activity of the central bank and the MPC contributes towards achieving a high and constant rate of economic growth.

Literature

Wiśniewski, Z. (2003): Labor market deregulation in the countries of the European Union, in: Frieske, K.W. (ed.), Polish labor market deregulation, Institute of Labor and Social Studies, Warsaw.

Assumptions of National Development Plan for 2007-2013. Warsaw, 30th April 2004.

National Development Plan, Warsaw, January 2003.

Kryńska, E. (2004): State on labor markets of an integrated Europe, in: Klamut, M. (ed.), Globalization process of the economy – the participation of the countries in advantages and costs of the process, Wroclaw University of Economics Publishers, Wroclaw.

NBP (2004a): Monetary policy guidelines for the year 2005, the MPC, Warsaw.

NBP (2004b): Monetary police instruments against the background of the liquidity of the bank sector in 2003, Warsaw.

NBP (2004c): Inflation report – November 2004, the MPC, Warsaw 2004.

Can Polish Monetary Policy Contribute to Mitigating the Unemployment Problem?

by

Maria Piotrowska

1 Conditions of the effective monetary policy

In the paper the ability of monetary policy to reduce the current high unemployment rate in Poland is investigated. Among economists there is almost a common opinion that monetary policy can influence a real economy at least in a short run. The changes in the monetary policy stance can be transmitted to the economy directly via banking system. Such a way of the monetary policy transmission is named the credit channel[1] and it is based on two principal assumptions: 1) supply of loans is sensitive to the changes in monetary policy, and 2) spending responds to changes in bank loan supply.

One should put stress that the central bank can only stimulate the behaviour of banks, however, they are independent in their portfolio decisions. In addition, if only minority of borrowers is dependent of bank loans, the changes in bank loan supply will have the weak impact on spending and unemployment. The effectiveness of monetary policy depends on a set of parameters which in most cases are not under control of the central banks. The monetary authority's actions can be a powerful tool to stimulate an economic growth and a decrease in unemployment in the short run, if other factors influencing bank lending support the mechanism of monetary policy transmission.

2 Factors affecting the efficiency of monetary policy

The following factors have been considered in the literature:[2]

1. **The exchange rate regime and the regulation of capital flows.** The fact that the central bank can control the money supply under floating exchange rates is one of the most important aspects of that exchange rate system. Under floating exchange rates, international capital flows increase the power of monetary policy.
2. **Labour market structure** determinates a degree of real wage "stickiness" that influences the monetary policy effectiveness.

---

1 Literature on the credit channel, see: Mishkin (1995), Bernanke and Gertler (1995) and Meltzer (1995).

2 Economic policy (1997), Mishkin (1995), Taylor (1995), Bernanke and Gertler (1995), Meltzer (1995).

3. **The financial structure.** The results obtained by Cottarelli and Kourelis (1995) pointed out that monetary policy impulses are transmitted to lending rates more rapidly:

   - when there are no constraints on bank competitions (in particular, barriers to entry);
   - when the banking system is privately owned;
   - when capital flows are perfectly liberalised;
   - when there is an efficient market for negotiable short-term instruments;
   - when random fluctuations in the money market rates are contained.

Kashyap and Stein (1997b, pp. 8-9), investigating a role of European banks in the monetary transmission mechanism, suggested that:

- In a country with a set of mostly creditworthy banks and relatively few bank-dependent firms, the lending channel effect would be fairly weak. In such a country, the banks might be able to offset the reduction in excess reserves by borrowing in the capital market. Moreover, most firms could continue spending even if bank loans were cut.
- On the contrary in a country with a weak banking system and many bank-dependent firms, the lending channel should work effectively. In this case, small banks that are usually less creditworthy, would not be able to find funds in the capital market to offset the contraction in reserves and they would have to cut their lending. Some their customers deprived of bank loans could not find other funding to finance their spending. Finally, a decline in production might occur.

Kashyap and Stein (1997a) as well as Gibson (1996) found the pattern:

- when the aggregate bank holdings of securities are low, lending is more responsive to monetary policy.

The impact of all factors, mentioned above, is important, however, a size of the paper forces to draw attention only to one of them. Taking into account very weak responses of Polish banks to the central bank actions carried out during recession in 2001-2002, investigating the impact of some financial structure characteristics seems to be justifiable.

3 The impact of financial structure on monetary policy in Poland

The relevance of financial structure to the efficiency of monetary policy in Poland should be assessed on the ground of two criteria:

- The ability of Polish banks to modify their credit policy in response to the central bank's actions;
- The sensitiveness of Polish firms' spending to the changes in the credit market.

3.1 Determinants of Polish banks' sensitiveness to changes in monetary policy

It was assumed that the ability of Polish banks to respond to the central bank's actions should be determined by the following factors:

- The level of concentration in banking system, measured by:
  - concentration ratios,
  - Herfindahl-Hirschman ratio;
- The financial condition of banks, measured by:
  - ROA, ROE
  - bank solvency index,
  - ratio of bad loans to total bank loans to the private sector
- The relevance of deposits as a source of loan funds;
- The share of securities in total bank assets.

The level of concentration in banking system

The consolidation process should draw a special attention because too high level of concentration can result in the reduction in the competition in the banking sector and finally in an increase in costs of financial services.

Table 1: The share of 5 largest banks* in net assets of banking sector in Poland and some chosen countries (in %)

	1995	2000	2001	2002	2003
Poland		**48.3**	**57.1**	**56.2**	**52.3**
Spain		54.0	53.0	53.0	
Greece		65.0	66.0	67.0	
Portugal		59.0	60.0	60.0	
Czech					65.7
Hungary					52.1
Slovakia					72.2
Slovenia					66.4
Netherlands	81.0				
Belgium	59.0				
Italy	29.0				
Germany	17.0				

Source: NBP (2004b), p. 74 and Kashyap / Stein (1997b), p. 9.

The level of concentration, measured by the share of 5 largest banks in net assets of banking sector, is presented in Table 1. In Poland the 5 largest banks held more than 50% of banking sector assets. How to interpret such a result. For example, Kashyap and Stein (1997b), investigating a role of European banks, evaluated that the large banks held a dominant position in the Netherlands and Belgium, while in Italy and Germany the smaller banks controlled a significant fraction of the assets. Therefore, under this criterion the level of concentration in Poland can be considered high. If five banks control 50% and ten banks 80%[3] of total banking assets, one should not expect that the competition in banking sector is very strong and the majority of costumers can find the loan costs low and the access to loans easy.

The concentration level of banking sector can be also measured by the Herfindahl-Hirschman ratio (HH)[4]. The interpretation of this ratio is as follows:

- $HH < 0.10$ low concentration
- $0.11 < HH < 0.18$ moderate concentration
- $HH > 0.18$ high concentration

The ratios in Poland in March 2002 were as follows:[5]

- for net assets HH = 0.0812
- for loans HH = 0.0707
- for deposits HH = 0.1085

Summarising, the Herfindahl-Hirschman ratio reveals that concentration is approaching to the moderate level, while the concentration ratios suggest that in Poland the large banks control a significant fraction of bank services. Making the final conclusion that the large banks have a dominant position in Poland, it was taken into account that 60 commercial banks held in 2003 95% of total banking assets while 600 co-operative banks only 5%.

Taking into account the ownership structure, since 1999 the private banks controlled by foreign investors have presented the strongest position. In 2003 their share in total banking assets was equal to 67.8%, (number of banks controlled by foreign investors amounted to 47).[6]

The financial condition of banks

The measures of the bank profitability and efficiency show that since 2003, after the recession, the financial condition of banks has started improving (see Table 2).

---

[3] Source: NBP (2002), Table 10, p. 35.

[4] $HH = \Sigma w_i^2$, where: w_i - the share of the i-bank in total assets or total loans or total deposits.

[5] Source: NBP (2002), Figure 3, p. 12.

[6] Source: NBP (2004b), p. 54.

Table 2: Measures of profitability and efficiency of banking sector (in %)

	2001	2002	2003	VI 2004
Net profit from assets (ROA)	1.0	0.5	0.5	0.75
Net profit from capital (ROE)	12.1	5.8	6.8	
Operating costs/assets	4.0	3.9	3.8	
Net interest income/assets (NIM)	3.7	3.4	3.1	
Bad loans/total loans	18.6	21.4	20.9	17.0
Operating costs/assets - EU 2002 - 2%				
Net interest income/assets : Spain 2002 - 2.64% Germany 2002 - 1.14%				
Bad loans/total loans - EU 2002 - 3.1%				

Source: NBP (2004b), Table 5.1.25, p. 70-72 and NBP (2004a).

The data published recently by the Polish central bank have revealed that in 2004 a number of banks with the lowest profitability (it means with ROA below 0.5% and ROE below 5%) as well as their share in banking sector assets considerably declined.[7]

However, operating costs in Polish banks were still relatively high in comparison to EU countries. It holds good for an interest margin that was twice higher than in Germany. It makes borrowing in Poland too costly for many firms.

The quality of loan portfolio is not satisfying. The share of bad loans is too high, especially if it is taken account that lost loans are a half of total bad loans. One should consider whether the 17% ratio of bad loans is the alarming signal. For comparison, during recession in Finland (1991-1993) and in Norway (1988-1992) bad loans amounted to 9% of total loans, and in Sweden (1991-1993) – 11%.[8] The data cannot be directly referred to Poland because there are no common international classification criteria of loans with the lowered quality. However, they point at the relevance of the problem. The quality of the loan portfolio in Poland is considerably lower than in EU countries. Taking into account that in EU countries the share of bank loans in GDP is much higher than in Poland, (in the EU, on average in 2000, 91%[9], while in Poland only 27.4%[10] in 2001), danger seems to be not so serious, however, such a high level of bad loans increases bank costs and discourages them to reduce lending rates,

---

7 Source: NBP (2004a), p. 29.

8 Source: BIS (1999), p.20.

9 Source: Deutsche Bank Research (2001), p. 8.

10 Source: NBP (2002), Table 7, p. 34 and Table 41, p. 54.

moreover, it induces them to tighten the credit conditions and finally it makes the access to funds much more difficult for many borrowers.

What is invigorative that recently the banking sector has not been in danger of insolvency. The average bank solvency index was above 8% in 2003 and 2004 – see Table 3 (even during the recession in 2001-2002 the solvency index was at the level 14%[11]). In 2004 there were very favourable shifts in the distribution of bank assets. The majority of banking sector assets belonged to banks with the solvency index at the level between 12% and 20%.[12] It means that the high level of own capital enabled banking sector to absorb losses which could occurred.

Table 3: Bank solvency index

	XII 2003	***VI 2004***
Average solvency index (%)	*13.8*	*15.6*

Source: NBP (2004a), Table 13, p. 28.

The relevance of deposits as a source of loan funds

In general, banks gather loan funds from four sources: deposits, borrowing in the interbank money market, borrowing from a central bank and issuing own securities. The dominant role of deposits makes monetary policy more efficient. If a central bank wants to stimulate a growth of loan supply, it can decline reserve requirements what it results in an increase in bank funds.

In Polish banks deposits are the main source of the funds. Considering commercial banks, in 2003 the share of private sector deposits in total liabilities was equal to 60%, while the share of borrowing in the interbank market amounted only to 15.5% and the share of borrowing from the central bank – 0.5%.[13] Therefore, borrowing in the interbank market did not contributed considerably to loan funds even in commercial banks, among which there were 15 largest banks. However the proportion between the share of deposits and the share of borrowing in the interbank market can be changed in the future. There are smaller foreign-owned banks that are not used deposits and they finance only by funds from their foreign owners and in the interbank market. If a number of such banks increase the relevance of deposits will decline. Issuing own securities by banks can be an additional source of the funds. However, in Poland it has not been a significant source yet – only 1.1%.

Therefore, the structure of fund sources in Polish banks is able to support loosening monetary policy.

---

[11] Source: NBP (2002), Table 30, p. 47.

[12] Source: NBP (2004a), p. 30.

[13] The share of private sector deposits in total liabilities of commercial banks is 61.4%, while the share of public sector deposits is 4.1%. Source: NBP (2002), Table 9, p. 34 and 54.

Table 5: Structure of liabilities in commercial banks (in %)

	2001	2002	2003
Borrowing from central bank	1.0	0.6	0.5
Deposits of private sector	61.7	57.8	59.8
Borrowing in interbank market	14.7	13.4	15.5
Deposits of government institutions	3.4	4.1	3.9
Issue of own securities	0.6	0.8	1.1

Source: NBP (2004b), Table 5.1.8. p. 58.

The share of securities in total bank assets

Banks can use their securities portfolios as a buffer that lets them respond to changes in monetary policy inconsistently with the central bank intentions. A central bank, reducing bank excess reserves, wants to induce banks to decline loan supply, however, banks can sell their securities to continue lending at the same level in the situation when they find lending profitable for them. Finally, restrictive monetary policy will be inefficient. If a central bank wants to stimulate the economic activity and increases bank excess reserves, it expects banks to extend loan supply, however, banks can use considerable part of the rise in excess reserves to buy securities when returns on securities are attractive in comparison to profits from lending. In such a situation expansionary monetary policy will not lead to the increase in loan supply sufficiently to incite the economic growth. Therefore, the theory predicts that low bank holdings of securities makes lending more responsive to monetary policy.

Table 6: Shares of lending and securities in total bank assets

*Share of private sector **lending** in total bank assets (in %)*

	Commercial banks	Co-operative banks
2001	42.3	52.1
2002	43.3	53.8
2003	44.5	57.2

*Share of **securities** in total bank assets (in %)*

	Commercial banks	Co-operative banks
2001	21.0	4.7
2002	23.5	5.6
2003	24.1	7.4

Source: NBP (2004b).

In Poland there was a considerable difference in the share of securities in total assets between commercial banks (24% in 2003) and co-operative banks, (only 7%)-see Table 6. One should immediately notice that commercial banks revealed lower lending ability than co-operative banks. In 2003 the share of loans to private sector in commercial banks was equal to 44.5% of total assets, while in co-operative banks – 57%.

Considering the structure of securities portfolios in commercial banks, government securities held the dominant position.[14] The share of different types of government securities in bank securities portfolios amounted to 62.1% in March 2002, when the recession still lasted. Banks found government securities very attractive. These free-risk securities gave the profitability at the level only a little lower than loans. Among the nine largest banks in March 2002, the seven of them offered one–year loans to firms at the average level of the interest rate equal to 10.82%, while at the same time the average interest rate on T-bills reached the level of 9.76%. Therefore, the interest rate spread was equal approximately only one percentage point.

During the recession of 2001-2002, commercial banks were inclined to use the funds obtained from the central bank, (via open market operations, the reductions in the reserve requirements or direct borrowing from the central bank), to buy government securities rather than to extend loans to risky customers. The response of banks to the reduction in reserve requirements can illustrate bank preferences. At the beginning of 2002, the central bank reduced reserve requirements from 5% to 4.5%. It resulted in an increase in bank free funds (excess reserves) by 7.8 PLN, of which 7.7 PLN banks invested in securities, mainly government securities.[15]

3.2 Summary of financial structure factors

The large banks have reached a relatively dominant position in Polish banking system. It has tended to limit the competition in the credit market and resulted in too high operating costs and too high interest margin. After the EU accession the financial service market in Poland should become more competitive.

In general, the levels of bank profitability and solvency have met the criteria of bank health. Strong banks would be able to take risk to extend considerably loan supply. Will they make such a decision? It will depend, on the one hand, on the credibility of costumers, and on the other hand, on the attractiveness of investment in government securities. As long as the public sector deficit remains at the high level and results in high supply of government securities, commercial banks are not interested in extending loans to risky customers.

The dominant position of deposits, as a source of bank funds, is conducive to the effective performance of lending channel. The reduction in reserve requirements can be a strong incidence to the increase in loan supply, however under condition, that exempted funds will not be invested in securities. The

---

[14] Source: NBP (2002).

[15] Source: NBP (2002).

summary of factors, that affect monetary policy in Poland, is presented in Table 7.

Table 7: Summary of factors affecting monetary policy in Poland

	Transmission of loosening monetary policy through banking system		
Factors	**Weak transmission**	**Moderate transmission**	**Strong transmission**
The level of concentration in banking system – DOMINANT POSITION OF RELATIVELY LARGE BANKS	X Because: - competition is not strong - too high operating costs - too high interest margin		
The financial condition of banks – IMPROVING		X Banks can take risk to extend loan supply	
The relevance of deposits as a source of loan funds – A DOMINANT SOURCE			X A decline in reserve requirements increases loan funds
The share of securities in total bank assets – HIGH	X Securities absorb bank funds – declining ability of banks to lend		However, sale of securities can increase loan funds, supporting loosening monetary policy

3.3 The sensitiveness of Polish firms' spending to the changes in monetary policy

The second criterion of the lending channel efficiency is the sensitiveness of firms' spending to the changes in monetary policy. If monetary policy is to contribute to the reduction in unemployment, investment must be sensitive to changes in interest rates or changes in loan supply. Is this criterion met in Poland? It seems that facts do not testify to it.

Since 2001 interest rates have tended to lower, moreover, since 2003 firms have used their capacity at the level higher than 78% (in 2004 in 81%) and nevertheless a rate of investment growth has remained negative until the third quarter of 2003. Investment started increasing only in 2004 and in fact the growth was really visible in the first half of the year.

Since 2003 the financial condition of firms has improved. In 2004 a profitability ratio was equal to 6.5%. It was the highest value in a history of the Polish market economy. Liquidity ratios in firms have also increased considerably. The good financial condition has improved the credibility of firms but it has not encouraged them to borrow from banks to invest. Firms have increased only their deposits in banks.[16]

The facts, mentioned above, suggest that the lower interest rate is not an important factor affecting investment decisions made by strong firms.

On the other hand in Poland the small and medium-size firms could be very strongly dependent of bank loans what it would make them very sensitive to changes in monetary policy. Taking into account that such firms produce 50% of GDP and create 70% of employment, they could be a channel through monetary policy reduces unemployment. They could be but they are not, because 90% of them do not use bank loans in their financing.[17] There are the following causes of it:

- Banks prefer large firms and in many cases their products are not suitable for small and medium-size firms;
- Interest rates are too high. On the contrary to large firms, investment decisions made by small and medium size firms are sensitive to the level of an interest rate.
- Collateral requirements are too restrictive for such firms. The relatively high level of bad loans induce banks to require very creditworthy collaterals. This problem could be solved by the special funds that offer credit guarantees for small and medium-size firms. In such a way the similar problem was solved in Spain. However in Poland there are only 50 such funds and the level of their capital is too low to give credit guarantees for all firms which need them.

4 Conclusions

In Poland, in general, financial deepening is at the low level. The ratio of banking sector assets to GDP is only 60%, while in the euro area 275%.[18] Therefore, changes in bank lending cannot be a very significant force driving GDP. Moreover, there are some obstacles, mentioned in this paper, that make monetary policy a less effective tool in mitigating the unemployment problem. It seems that the Polish central bank will contribute to the reduction in unemployment if it remains in its primary objective, it means a low and stable

[16] Source: NBP (2004a), p. 4.
[17] Data published by Polska Agencja Rozwoju Przedsiebiorczosci.
[18] Source: NBP (2004b), pp. 55-56.

inflation rate. The principal economic rationale behind the price stability objective is that price stability contributes to an optimal allocation of production factors. Thus low and stable inflation should promote a sustainable high rate of economic growth and a high level of employment via low long-term interest rates.

Literature

BIS (1999): Bank Restructuring in Practice, in: BIS Policy Papers, No. 6 sierpień 1999.

Bernanke, B. and Gertler, M. (1995): Inside the Balack Box: The Credit Channel of Monetary Transmission Mechanism, in: Journal of Economic Perspectives, 9/4, pp. 27-49.

GUS (2001): Bilansowe wyniki finansowe podmiotów gospodarczych w 2000 r.

Carpenter, R.E., Fazzari, S.M. and Petersen, B. C. (1994): Inventory Investment , Internal-finance Fluctuations, and the Business Cycle, in: Brookings Papers on Economic Activity, pp. 75-138.

Deutsche Bank Research (2001): EU Enlargement Monitor. Central and Eastern Europe, sierpień 2001.

Gertler, M. and Gilchrist, S. (1994): Monetary Policy, Business Cycles, and the Behavior of Small Manufacturing Firms, in: Quarterly Journal of Economics, Vol. 109, maj 1994, pp. 309-340.

Gibson, M. (1996): The Bank Lending Channel of Monetary Policy Transmission: Evidence from a Model of Bank Behavior that Incorporates Long-term Customer Relationships, Federal Reserve Board, working paper.

Kashyap, A. K., Stein, J. C., and Lamont, O. (1994): Credit Conditions and the Cyclical Behavior of Inventories, Quarterly Journal of Economics, Vol. 109, sierpień, 1994.

Kashyap, A. K., and Stein, J. C. (1994): Monetary Policy and Bank Lending, in: Mankiew N. G. (ed.), Monetary Policy, pp. 221-256, Chicago.

Kashyap, A. K., and Stein, J. C. (1997a): What Do a Million Banks Have to Say about the Transmission of Monetary Policy, in: NBER Working Paper Series, No. 6056.

Kashyap, A. K., and Stein, J. C. (1997b): The Role of Banks in Monetary Policy: A Survey with Implications for the European Monetary Union, Economic Perspectives, wrzesień/październik, 1997, pp. 2-18.

Meltzer, A. H. (1995): Monetary, Credit (and Other) Transmission Processes: A Monetarist Perspective, in: Journal of Economic Perspectives, 9/4, pp. 49-72.

Mishkin, F. S. (1995): Symposium on Monetary Transmission Mechanism, in: Journal of Economic Perspectives, 9/4, pp. 3-10.

NBP (2001): Raport o stabilności systemu finansowego, styczeń 2000 – czerwiec 2001, pod red. M. Gołajewska, R. Kokoszczyński and Z. Polański, Warszawa, grudzień 2001.

NBP (2002): Sytuacja finansowa banków w I kwartale 2002 r. Synteza., Warszawa, lipiec 2002.

NBP (2004a): Przeglad stabilnosci systemu finansowego, I polrocze 2004, Warszawa 2004.

NBP (2004b): Rozwoj systemu finansowego w Polsce w latach 2002-2003, Warszawa, 2004.

Sharpe, S. A. (1995): Bank Capitalization, Regulation, and the Credit Crunch: A Critical review of the Research Findings, in: Federal Reserve Board Working Paper Series, no. 20/95.

Taylor, J. B. (1995): The Monetary Transmission Mechanism: An Empirical Framework, in: Journal of Economic Perspectives, 9/4, pp. 11-26.

Is investing abroad unpatriotic?[1]
Jobs and investment in an expanding EU

by

Aloys Prinz

1 Introduction

Recently, there has been a new dimension added to the discussion of globalisation and, especially, of the Eastern enlargement of the European Union (EU). This new dimension might be called the 'patriotic turn', not known in Germany in the past when questions of globalisation had been discussed. The argument may be summarized briefly as follows: It might be profitable and economically sound to invest abroad (and especially in EU member states), however, if this occurs at the cost of domestic job losses it is unpatriotic. Hence, a patriotic German firm is obliged to invest in Germany and to create jobs there even if there are more profitable alternatives outside Germany. It is obvious that this is an argument that questions the moral justification of investing abroad. However, the main intent of the argument seems to be to distract the public focus of attention from the shortcomings and problems of German economic policy and to redirect it to the behaviour of firms. Such strategic games are not at all new, and they are surely not well suited for a sound economic analysis. Since in this paper the economics of investing abroad shall be at stake, the political economy of blaming the different players with respect to the responsibility for economic problems will not be analysed here any further.[2] The reason is that the economic rationality of investing abroad and its effects on domestic employment seem much more interesting and much more difficult to answer.

The paper is organized as follows: In the next section, some facts concerning German foreign investments are presented. The most interesting question is why foreign investments take place; it is addressed in the third section of the paper. The specific effects of globalisation and especially the Eastern enlargement of the EU are analysed in section four. In section five, the dynamics of product cycles are incorporated to explain why a country might loose whole industries without generally losing jobs. The labour market consequences of investing abroad – taken into account the effects of globalisation – are analysed. The paper will be completed in section seven with some conclusions.

---

1 The title of this paper was inspired by the paper of Geishecker / Görg (2004a).

2 See, for instance, Die Zeit (2004), p. 21.

2 Facts on German FDIs

Foreign direct investments (FDIs) are not at all a new phenomenon. Generally, they are defined as follows:

> "International investment by a resident entity in one economy (direct investor; parent company; multinational) to acquire or set up a subsidiary (affiliate) in a foreign country and all subsequent capital transactions between the parent company and the foreign subsidiary and among the foreign subsidiaries part of the multinational (…)."[3]

This definition shows that FDIs encompass investments abroad without recurring to investment motives.

The capital stock abroad which is held by German firms (outward FDI[4]) amounted in the year 2000 to 570 billion Euro or 28% of the German GDP.[5] In 1995, the capital stock invested abroad was 10% of GDP.[6] In contrast, inward FDI[7] increased only from 7% of GDP in 1995 to 10% of GDP in 2000.[8] That means that German firms invested much more in foreign countries than firms from other countries invested in Germany. About 50% of all German FDIs (220 billion Euro) are in manufacturing.[9] Figure 1 shows the change in the stock of German FDIs[10] for the years 2000 to 2003 as a whole and differentiated according to groups of countries. Of special interest are the so-called reform countries[11]: German FDIs to these countries grew over this period substantially more than those to the other groups of countries. However, the total stock of German FDIs at the end of 2003 was largest in industrial countries (86.2%), followed by that in reform countries with 7%.[12]

---

3 Barba-Navaretti / Venables (forthcoming), Glossary "Foreign direct investment (FDI)".

4 See Barba-Navaretti / Venables (forthcoming), Glossary.

5 See Geishecker / Görg (2004a).

6 See Geishecker / Görg (2004a).

7 FDI from other countries in Germany; see Barba-Navaretti / Venables (forthcoming), Glossary.

8 See Geishecker / Görg (2004a).

9 See Geishecker / Görg (2004a).

10 "Unmittelbare und (über abhängige Holdinggesellschaften im Ausland bestehende) mittelbare deutsche Direktinvestitionen im Ausland (konsolidiert)"; Deutsche Bundesbank (2005), p. 16.

11 These countries are: Belarus, Bosnia and Herzegovina, Bulgaria, China, Estonia, Kazakhstan, Croatia, Latvia, Lithuania, Macedonia, Poland, Rumania, Russian Federation, Serbia and Montenegro, Slovakia, Slovenia, Czech Republic, Ukraine, Hungary and Uzbekistan.

12 Own calculations based on Deutsche Bundesbank (2005), pp. 16 ff.

Figure 1: German FDIs to groups of countries, 2000 – 2003

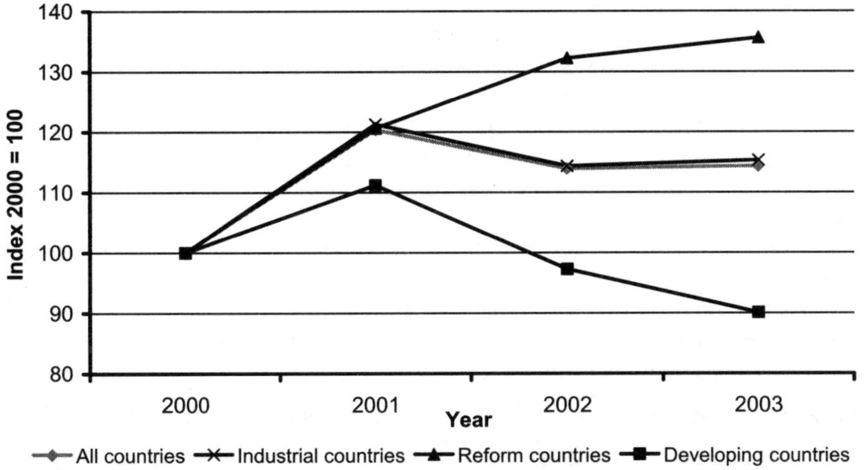

Source: Own calculations and depiction; data source: Deutsche Bundesbank (2005), pp. 16 ff.

Concerning Central and Eastern European Countries (CEECs), 5% of the German capital stock invested abroad is located in these countries.[13] 40% of this capital is invested in manufacturing (for comparison: 47% of the German capital invested in the US is also in manufacturing).[14]

To complete this overall picture, a summarizing quote from a recent study is presented:

> "We find that German investors transfer a substantial amount of financial capital to EE (Eastern Europe, A.P.) (...) We also find strong evidence that German corporations are outsourcing a substantial share of their production to EE affiliates to exploit lower wages in the East."[15]

It is clear that such results may cause tremendous fears in a country that is very short of jobs as Germany.

The importance of Germany as an investor in Eastern European Countries is depicted in Table 1. Especially for the Central East European Countries Germany seems to play a major role as a foreign investor. However, this is hardly surprising when a broader historical picture is taken into account: Before World War II, Germany was also a large investor in those countries. Insofar there is almost nothing new, and especially neither globalisation nor the EU access itself should be blamed for the German investment in those countries.

---

13 See Geishecker / Görg (2004a).

14 See Geishecker / Görg (2004a).

15 Marin / Lorentowicz / Raubold (2002), Abstract.

Removing the barriers for investment, some old patterns of investment strategies simply seem to re-emerge.

Given that the labour cost in Eastern Europe are between 37 to 73% lower than in Germany, it is not surprising that firms are mainly motivated for FDI in those countries by these lower costs.[16] Hence, outsourcing of labour intensive stages of production is the consequence. However, a rough calculation – taking account of different effects of job destruction as well as job creation – showed that Germany had to face a net job destruction of about 89.000 jobs – a low number.[17]

For the explanation of this result it is important to recognize that FDI serves often to outsource labour intensive stages of production. That implies, however, that a substantial part of the trade with Eastern Europe countries is intra-firm trade. Intermediate goods are imported within a multinational firm that sourced out stages of its manufacturing process.

Table 1: Importance of Germany as an investor in Eastern Europe, 1998-1999

Country	Share* (in %)	Country	Share* (in %)
Central Eastern Europe	**23.71**	**Southern Eastern Europe**	**n. a.**
Croatia	27.90	Bosnia & Herzegovina	16.90
Czech Republic	29.60	Bulgaria	8.00
Hungary	28.00	Romania	10.20
Poland	17.30	**Former Soviet Union**	**n. a.**
Slovak Republic	22.00	Belarus	25.00
Slovenia	12.30	Moldova	6.40
Baltic States	**4.01**	Russia	8.10
Estonia	2.50	Ukraine	8.30
Latvia	8.40		
Lithuania	2.00		

*: Share as % of worldwide inward FDI in the respective country.
Source: Marin / Lorentowicz / Raubold (2002), Table 1a, p. 5, on the basis of UNCTAD data.

90% of German East European investment in machinery and transport are outsourcing investments, but also 79% of investments in services are also of this type.[18] This gives rise to the fact that 11.67% of German total exports to Eastern

---

[16] See Marin (2004), p. 16.

[17] See Marin (2004), Table 7, p. 17, based on a survey of 2200 investment projects by 660 firms in Eastern Europe.

[18] See Marin (2004), Table 5, p. 12, based on survey data.

Europe and 21.56% of its total imports from those countries are intra-firm exports and imports, respectively.[19]

The question is, what it all does mean for the German economy. The fear that investing abroad instead of investing in Germany may be based on the fact that without an increase of domestic investments it is unlikely that many new jobs will be created. Figure 2 shows the plunge of net investment in% of NNP (net national product) in Germany in the years after 2000. This demonstrates that the German economy is in dire need of investments.

Figure 2: Net investment in % of NNP and the rate of unemployment in Germany, 1991-2002

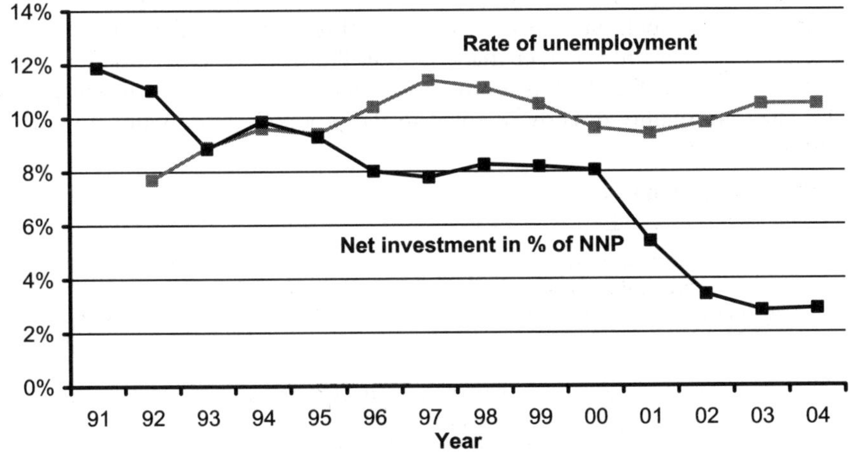

Source: Statistical appendix of SVR (2003) and SVR (2005), respectively.

3 Meaning and consequences of investing abroad

Both, export surpluses as well as FDI are a form of capital export. In contrast to export surpluses which are accompanied by the net outflow of domestic savings and the accumulation of wealth in foreign countries, FDI is an explicit investment strategy of home country firms to establish subsidiaries in the host country, buying firms abroad or moving the location of a firm to the host country. With FDI, two different forms are possible (see also Figure 3): horizontal and vertical direct investments.[20] Horizontal investments are mainly based on the following motives:[21]

---

[19] See Marin (2004), Table 6, p. 15, based on survey data.

[20] See Markusen (2004) and Markusen (2002).

[21] See Markusen (2004) and also Barba-Navaretti / Venables (forthcoming), chapter 2.

- opening up new markets as a substitute or a complement to exports,
- increasing the competitiveness of a firm by exploiting economies of scale and scope,
- gaining access to foreign capital markets,
- circumventing import restrictions of foreign countries and
- expanding the firm's activities as well as a measure of the customer relation management.[22]

Vertical foreign investments (VFDI)[23], also called outsourcing and offshoring, increase the world-wide division of labour by 'slicing up the value chain[24]' (Paul Krugman). The main reason is therefore increasing productivity by decreasing costs. Beside or in addition to that, with vertical investments abroad it may also be intended to open up markets for immobile factors of production (i.e. especially, but not only, labour markets). On the basis of this classification of FDIs, it is obvious that VFDIs are the most interesting and most recent part of FDI. They are mainly directly oriented to the production or supply side of the economy.

Figure 3: Location of industry

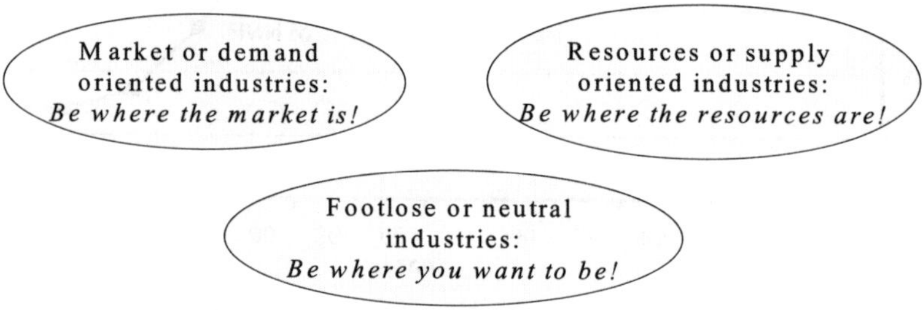

Source: Diagram based on Carbaugh (1992), pp. 91 f.

Applied to Germany, how do German firms fit into this picture? In a recent study of German companies, the following classification of firms with respect to the 'globalisation' of their activities was found:[25]

---

22 For a more complete explanation see Markusen (2004) and Barba-Navaretti / Venables (forthcoming), chapter 2.

23 "Foreign direct investment involving the transfer abroad of one or more of the firm's stages of production, generally in order to access low cost inputs and to use output to supply other parts of the multinational's operations by means of intra-firm exports"; Barba-Navaretti / Venables (forthcoming), Glossary "Vertical Foreign Direct Investment (VFDI)".

24 Also called 'fragmentation'; see for instance Geishecker / Görg (2004b) or Barba-Navaretti / Venables (forthcoming), Glossary.

25 Roland Berger (2004), p. 11.

1. 17% of the companies are called "German based value creators". Their manufacturing as well as R&D is based in Germany and they serve international customers via their home base.
2. 22% of the companies are called "regional cost cutters". They shift labour cost intensive stages of production to low cost countries in Eastern Europe and East Asia.
3. 33% of the companies are called "global market experts". They maintain local manufacturing and sales locations for serving international markets.
4. 28% of the companies are called "global footprint champions". The different corporate functions are located where it seems best and they form together a global network.

This seems to imply that those 22% of the firms that are classified as "regional cost cutters" are the main investors in VFDI. If this is correct, these firms must be heavily engaged in offshoring and outsourcing activities that are regarded by politicians as dangerous to German jobs and that are called 'unpatriotic'. However, what does economic theory tell us – if anything – about the location *dynamics*, or put differently, is the Eastern enlargement of the EU or globalisation indeed to blame for low investments and high unemployment in Germany?

4 Product life cycles and location dynamics

To understand the interdependence of the location dynamics of industries and the life cycle of products, consider a product that is produced with a relative high labour intensity in the home country.[26] Since the product is a success in the home country as well as in foreign markets, the domestic production expands and the domestic industry shows export strength. However, as a reaction to the export success foreign production is taken up and the industry in the home country loses its competitive advantage. Import competition emerges and the position of domestic production is weakened.

How can the domestic industry react in this process? When expanding its production, domestic wages increase. The increase of labour costs can be countered by employing more capital. The more competitive foreign production becomes, the higher the cost pressure on domestic production gets. To counter that, the most labour-intensive stages of production will be outsourced to low-wages countries where the costs of transportation are low and the quality of the production fits the requirements of the domestic industry. However, the further increase of product quality in import competition in combination with further increasing wages in the home country will finally drive the domestic industry

[26] See for the following scenario Carbaugh (1992), p. 76.

out of business, i.e. the entire manufacturing process moves to other countries. Only high-tech and high-price variants of the product have a chance to be produced in the home country. In the end, the world-wide division of labour and specialisation has increased.

It is quite easy to recognise that 'slicing up the value chain' or 'fragmentation of production' is embedded in the world-wide process of division of labour. This process gets a higher momentum if there are no toll barriers and if there is a single market. The EU is providing both in its member states. Admitting new member states to the EU is therefore likely to speed up the division of labour among the countries involved. It is clear that the speeding up of the division of labour will force further structural changes in the economies involved. Since Germany is the nearest as well as the biggest economy of the former EU that is neighbouring the new Eastern Europe member states it is to be conjectured that Germany will have to face the major burden of adjustment.[27] It is also obvious that the German labour market will have to adjust to the new developments, and that at a time when this market itself is in dire of reform. In a sense, a new spectre is haunting Germany, if not Europe: the factor price equalization theorem.[28] According to this well-known theorem, international trade will lead sooner or later to the same wage rates (as well as interest rates) all over Europe (or even the world).

In the next section the labour market consequences of the dynamic adjustments of manufacturing operations in the enlarged EU will be analysed.

5 Labour market effects of outsourcing

5.1 General aspects

To analyse the labour market effects of outsourcing, a special analytical tool, namely the Factor Price Frontier (FPF), will be used. The FPF was developed in 1962 as a surrogate production function by transforming the isoquant of the production function into a kind of iso-cost function.[29] The construction of the FPF via the production function is shown in Figure 4. In this figure, the following notation is used: K capital, L labour, Y output, p output price, w wage rate, r interest rate, f(…) production function, c(…) iso-cost curve, w(…) wage function.

---

[27] Sinn (2003) therefore called the Eastern enlargement of the EU "the second reunification that western Germany has experienced within a short period of time".

[28] See also Sinn (2003).

[29] See Samuelson (1962).

Figure 4: Derivation of the Factor Price Frontier from the production function

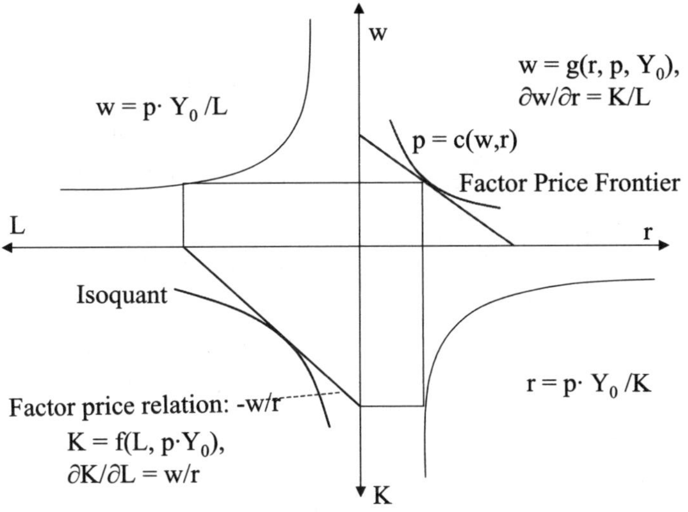

Source: Lang (1983), p. 368 (slightly modified).

Starting with the rewritten production function $K = f(L, pY_0)$ in the third quadrant in Figure 3, the optimal employment of labour and capital results for given factor prices w and r at the point where the isoquant is tangent to the budget restriction. At this point, the optimal capital-labour ratio under the given circumstances is determined. Projecting this via the second and fourth quadrant on the first quadrant and using the given factor prices defines a point of the FPF. The slope of the wage function $w = g(r, p, Y_0)$ with respect to r yields the capital-labour ratio (the capital intensity of production).

The FPF analysis can be used to determine the effects of outsourcing mentioned in section 4 of this paper.[30] The results of this analysis are shown in Figure 5.

[30] Kohler (2003, 2004) uses FPF analysis as a tool to study the effects of outsourcing in a much more elaborated microeconomic framework. The analysis presented in the following is much simpler than that of Kohler.

Figure 5: Factor Price Analysis of outsourcing

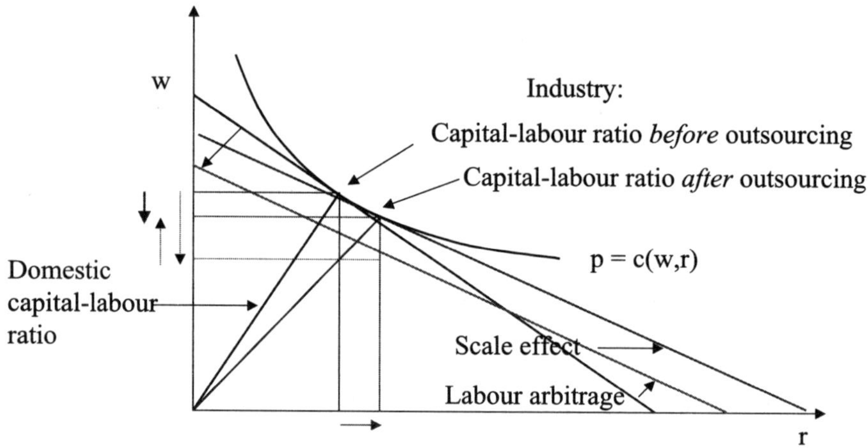

Source: Own depiction.

The point of departure in Figure 4 is the FPF with the capital-labour ratio of the firm under consideration *before* outsourcing. The iso-cost curve p = c(w, r) determines combinations of the wage rate and the interest rate that leave the costs of production constant. This implies that the price on the market for the good under consideration, p, is given, i.e. the firm is a price taker on the goods market. The iso-cost curve c(w, r) determines all combinations of w and r for which the costs of production do not exceed the market price.

Assume now that – e.g. due to the Eastern enlargement of the EU – the firm gains access to low-wage countries and becomes able to outsource labour intensive stages of the manufacturing process. This opens up new ways for cutting production costs via labour arbitrage. This is depicted in Figure 5 by turning around and shifting inward the wage function. The turning of the wage function is due to the fact that for the domestic firm the relevant factor price relation has changed in the direction of lower wages. In addition to that, outsourcing labour intensive stages of the manufacturing process to low-wage countries reduces the production cost as a whole via the dismissal of domestic high-wage workers. This will trigger a second effect – a scale effect. Given that the market price of the good does not change, this allows the firm to pay higher rewards to its domestic factors of production.[31] This is shown in Figure 5 by shifting the new wage curve outward until it is tangent to the given iso-cost curve.

In this way the capital-labour ratio has changed, i.e. the production as a whole becomes less capital intensive as before despite the fact that the domestic

[31] See also Kohler (2004), p. C167.

capital-labour ratio does not necessarily change. It is obvious that the labour arbitrage effect of outsourcing puts a heavy burden on domestic labour in the home country. However, this negative effect is partially countered and offset by the scale effect. Both effects taken together might imply that domestic labour has to bear a burden (at least temporally), but the burden might not be as high as it seems at first glance.

Empirical evidence shows that in the recent past an 1% increase of outsourcing activities led to a decline of low-skill wages by 1.8%, but to an increase of high-skill wages by 3%.[32] This sheds some light on the real problems of the German labour market. High-skill labour is rather scarce and profits from the internationalisation of firms and production. Low-skill labour on the other hand, however, seems to come more and more under pressure, be it via globalisation or by the expansion of the EU. Therefore it is necessary to have a closer look at the special problems of this sector of the German labour market.

5.2 Specific aspects for low-skill labour

To understand the effects of EU expansion as well as globalisation on low-skill labour it is necessary to know the specific adjustment patterns of this part of the German labour market. The adjustment patterns are shown in Figure 6.

Figure 6: Migration patterns between industry and services in Germany

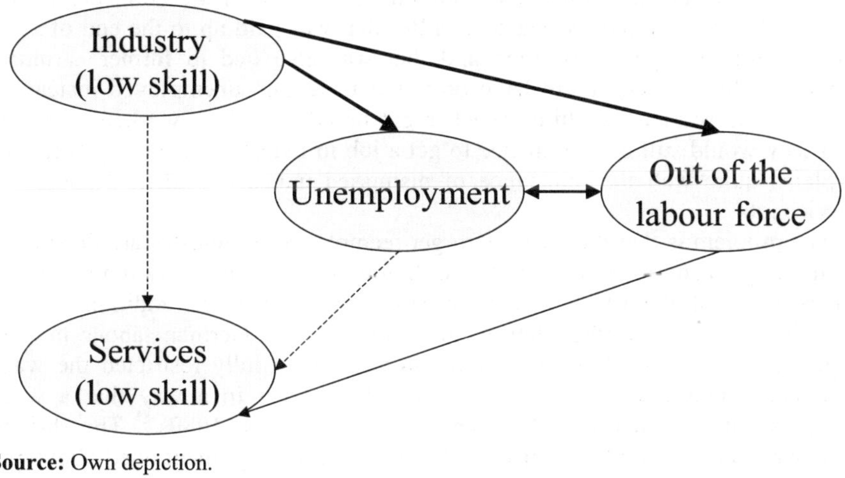

Source: Own depiction.

The most important fact is that workers who lost their jobs in the industrial sector of the German economy did in the recent past rarely migrate to the service

---

[32] See Geishecker / Görg (2004b).

sector.[33] Rather than to migrate to services they became unemployed and remained so for quite a long time, or they left the labour force (via early retirement programmes etc.). The service sector, on the other hand, recruited its labour force to a very large extent from persons that entered the labour force and went directly to this sector. As a result, employment in the service sector (in percent of total employment) is in Germany lower than in other comparable countries.

The crucial question is, however, what deters workers who become unemployed in the industrial sector from migration to the service sector? One explanation could be that the skills of industrial (low-skill) workers do not fit the requirements of the service sector. This explanation is not convincing since in other countries the skill differences between sectors will be as high as in Germany. It may take a certain time to prepare industrial workers for a service job, but the necessary retraining may be completed in relatively short time. More likely is that the wage differential between the industrial and the service sector is rather large in Germany. The explanation rests on the fact that the German industry produces capital intensive whereas the service sector is much less capital intensive. Migrating from industry to services is then accompanied by a rather large wage decline. In addition to that the high industry wages entitle dismissed workers to high unemployment benefits since these benefits are related to the former earnings. Combining this fact with a second tier unemployment benefit called 'Arbeitslosenhilfe' that was paid up to the end of 2004 for an unlimited period of time and that was also tied to former earnings, explains why workers might have preferred to remain unemployed instead of migrating to services. A third aspect might be added: Many workers expected that they would still have a chance to get a job in industry. Taken together, this explains quite well the reluctance of dismissed industry workers to accept a service job.

The problem is that the chances to get reemployed in industry are drastically reduced by outsourcing low-skill labour to low-wage countries. With the Eastern enlargement of the EU they are virtually non existent. In addition to that, globalisation has a further detrimental effect for the German labour market, especially in its low-skill area. Trade unions successfully restricted the wage differential between high-skill and low-skill workers in a way that a wage compression was created in Germany in the 1970s and 1980s.[34] The shift of labour demand in combination with the structural change mentioned above put the low-wage sector under heavy pressure. However, there was no substantial change of the wages of low-skill workers. Since these wages were set too high

---

[33] See for this and the following Klodt (2004).

[34] See Prasad (2004) as well as Schöb / Weimann (2003).

in relation to the wages of high-skill workers, Germany developed a serious unemployment problem with low-skill workers.[35]

Figure 7: Globalisation and structural adjustment

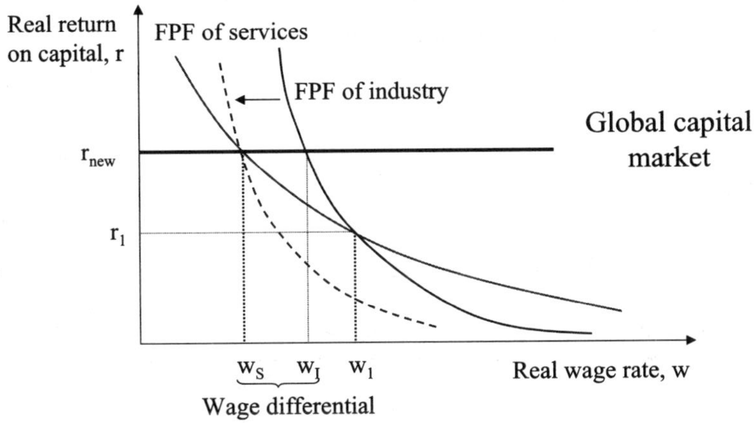

Source: Own depiction using a method of Krugman / Obstfeld (1994), p. 84.

Given this situation on the low-skill labour market, what effect globalisation will have? Globalisation is identified here with open international capital markets, implying very mobile capital flows. Consequently, the rate of return on investments is by and large determined on the international capital market. This implies that a redistribution of income from capital to labour is no longer feasible. This will have serious consequences for the industrial sector as well as the labour market of low-skill workers, as depicted in Figure 7 and Figure 8.

In Figure 7, FPF analysis is applied again to explain the globalisation effect on structural adjustment between industry and services.[36] Instead of one FPF for the whole economy, two different FPFs are shown that represent the industrial and the service sector, respectively. An equilibrium is reached at the intersections of the FPFs. It is assumed that as a starting point an equilibrium existed at r_1, w_1. Globalisation as interpreted here changed the distribution between capital and labour to the advantage of capital; a return on investment of r_{new} is assumed to be required now to get capital from the international capital market. This requirement creates a wage differential between the industrial and the service sector since the industry is able to pay a higher wage because its labour productivity is higher than that of services. However, left to market forces this

---

[35] See Prinz (2004) for a more comprehensive analysis.

[36] Note, however, that for ease of depiction the axes are interchanged: w is on the abscissa, r is on the ordinate.

wage differential is not sustainable and, hence, no equilibrium. Outsourcing of low-skill labour puts industrial wages under pressure until an equilibrium is eventually reached with identical wages for identical (low-skill) labour at the lower of both wage levels, i.e. the wage level of the service sector.

Figure 8: Globalisation and the labour market

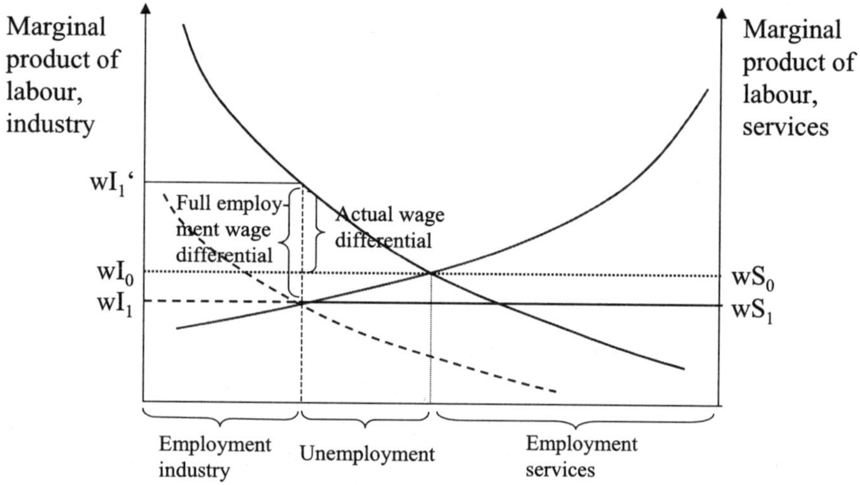

Source: Own depiction.

The consequences for the labour market are shown in Figure 8. On both ordinates, the marginal product of labour of the sectors is depicted whereas the distance between the vertical axes is the labour force of the home country. The diagram shows an equilibrium of the labour market that consists of two sectors, industry and services. Initially there is assumed to be an equilibrium without unemployment and the same wage for low-skill labour in both sectors. Outsourcing of labour-intensive stages of manufacturing shifts the labour demand curve of the industry to the left. A new full-employment equilibrium would require that the wages of both sectors had to decline. Assume now that due to the bargaining power of trade unions the industry wage increases to wI_1' and the wage in the service sector stays where it started, namely at wS_0. The actual wage differential in Figure 8 is, then, not sufficient to create full employment. However, even if the wage differential were large enough, this would not establish an equilibrium because the same quality of labour would demand two different prices. A new full-employment equilibrium requires a single wage rate of $wI_1 = wS_1 < wI_0 = wS_0$. In this new equilibrium, the adjustment to the structural change is completed and the number of workers in the service sector has increased, accompanied by a decrease of jobs in industry.

This structural change will cause further serious problems for the German labour market. Until now the structural change triggered by changes in the 1970s and 1980s are still incomplete in Germany; the Eastern enlargement of the EU, combined with the more general capital market effects of globalisation will increase the pressure on the German labour market. Policy makers are well advised to react rather quickly to make the German labour market fit for these adjustment processes.

6 Conclusions

In this paper, some economic aspects of investing abroad and its consequences for the domestic labour market are analysed. The Eastern enlargement of the EU opened up the door for outsourcing labour intensive stages of the manufacturing process using the low wages of the accession countries. In a sense, the EU expansion intensified the general globalisation effects, especially for Germany.

Employing a well-known analytical tool, Factor Price Frontier Analysis, it is explained how firms can benefit from the EU's Eastern expansion and what consequences are to be expected. As a result, it is shown that the capital intensity of production will change and that the factors of production will disproportionately benefit from EU expansion. However, it is to be guessed that the redistribution effect between the factors of production will not be as large as feared.

Furthermore it is analysed how structural change is enforced by globalisation and what consequences this might have for the German labour market. The result was that a further increase of the service sector at the cost of a decreasing industrial sector is to be expected. This will intensify the pressure on the labour market especially for low-skill labour. Without quick reforms of the labour markets even more serious employment problems are to be expected in this part of the labour market.

Literature

Barba-Navaretti, G. and Venables, A.J. (forthcoming): Multinational firms in the world economy, forthcoming Princeton University Press.

Carbaugh, R.J. (1992): International economics, 4th ed., Wadsworth: Belmont, Ca.**Deutsche Bundesbank (2005):** Kapitalverflechtung mit dem Ausland, April 2005, Frankfurt a. M.

Die Zeit (2004): Die Arbeit wandert aus, in: Die Zeit, 07.04.2004, p. 21.

Geishecker, I. and Görg, H. (2004a): Investitionen deutscher Unternehmen im Ausland: Mangelnder Patriotismus?, in: Wochenbericht des DIW Berlin 42/04.

Geishecker, I. and Görg, H (2004b): Winners and losers: Fragmentation, trade and wages revisited (updated version), DIW Berlin, Discussion Papers 385.

Klodt, H. (2004): Strukturwandel und Arbeitsmarktprobleme in Deutschland, in: Die Weltwirtschaft, 3/2004, pp. 301-316.**Kohler, W. (2004):** International outsourcing and factor prices with multistage production, in: The Economic Journal, vol. 114 (March), pp. C166-C185.

Kohler, W. (2003): The distributional effects of international fragmentation, in: German Economic Review, vol. 4, pp. 89-120.

Krugman, P.R. and Obstfeld, M. (1994): International Economics: Theory and Policy, 3rd ed., HarperCollins: New York. **Lang, F.P. (1983):** Supply-Side-Economics und „Factor-Price-Frontier“, in: wisu (Das Wirtschaftsstudium), vol. 12 (1983), p. 366-372.**Marin, D. (2004):** 'A nation of poets and thinkers' – Less so with Eastern enlargement? Austria and Germany, Discussion paper 2004-06, Department of Economics, University of Munich.

Marin, D., Lorentowicz, A. and Raubold, A. (2002): Ownership, capital or outsourcing: What drives German investment to Eastern Europe?, Discussion Paper 02-03, Department of Economics, University of Munich.

Markusen, J. (2004): Regional integration and third-country inward investment, in: Business and Politics, vol. 6, issue 1, article 3, Internet resource: URL: http://www.bepress.com/bap/vol6/iss1/art3 [08.12.2004].

Markusen, J.R. (2002): Multinational firms and the theory of international trade, Cambridge, Mass.: MIT Press.

Prasad, E.S. (2004): The unbearable stability of the German wage structure: Evidence and interpretation, in: IMF Staff Papers, vol. 51, pp. 354-385.

Prinz, A. (2004): Reform der Arbeitsmarktpolitik: Alter Wein in neuen Schläuchen?, in: Perspektiven der Wirtschaftspolitik, vol. 5, pp. 313-332.

Roland Berger Strategy Consultants (2004): Global footprint design – Mastering the rules of international value creation. Study. Munich, June 2004.

Samuelson, P.A. (1962): Parable and realism in capital theory: The surrogate production function, in: Review of Economic Studies, vol. 29, pp. 193 -206.

Schöb, R. and Weimann, J. (2003): Arbeit ist machbar: die neue Beschäftigungsformel, Dößel.

Sinn, W. (2003): Another unification and more illusions, Ifo Viewpoint Munich, January 8, 2003.

SVR (2003): Sachverständigenrat zur Begutachtung der gesamtwirtschaftlichen Entwicklung, Staatsfinanzen konsolidieren – Steuersystem reformieren, Jahresgutachten 2003/04, Berlin.

SVR (2005): Sachverständigenrat zur Begutachtung der gesamtwirtschaftlichen Entwicklung, Die Chancen nutzen – Reformen mutig voranbringen, Jahresgutachten 2005/06, Berlin.

Skill-biased technical change and structural unemployment in Europe

by

Thomas Apolte

1 Wage gap and unemployment in Europe and the United States

In the United States as well as in Great Britain, an increased spread in wages of high skilled and low skilled employees has been observed since some 15 to 20 years now. At the same time, the number of high skilled employees has increased more than employment of low skilled. Finally, the overall rate of unemployment decreased both in the United States and in Great Britain. The fact that the rate of vacancies did not decrease to the same extend as the rate of unemployment indicates that structural unemployment decreased in these countries. Technically speaking, we can observe a move along a given Beveridge curve rather than an inward shift of that curve. This fits into the results of estimations of the non accelerating inflation rate of unemployment (NAIRU), according to which the NAIRU decreased both in the United States and in Great Britain over the 1990s.

In continental Europe, and here especially in Germany, France, and Italy, the picture is remarkably different. Here, the spread between high skilled and low skilled workers is not as pronounced as in the US and in Great Britain. At the same time, we observe a more or less steady increase in unemployment, especially of low skilled persons. Moreover, not only has overall unemployment increased but also long-term unemployment and structural unemployment. The latter is indicated both by outward shifts in the Beveridge curve and by estimates of the NAIRU.

For any given dynamic of supply and demand for skilled and unskilled workers, the differences between the US and the UK on the one hand and large parts of continental Europe on the other hand can be explained by differences in labour-market adaptability. Labour markets and especially wage structures have traditionally been more flexible in the US than in Europe, and UK labour markets have become considerably more flexible since the deregulation policy of the "iron lady" Margaret Thatcher. By contrast, labour markets and wage structures in continental Europe have traditionally been more rigid, and they have become increasingly so over the last thirty years. Under such conditions, structural shifts in demand for labour lead to unemployment rather than to deeper spreads in wages.

Economists have little arguments about the differences in the picture between the US and the UK on the one hand and continental Europe on the other. Rather, they have been struggling for a proper explanation of the underlying structural shifts in labour demand. Obviously, there has been an outward shift in demand for (highly) skilled labour whereas, at the same time, there was an inward shift in demand for low or unskilled labour. This can be illustrated by a simple graphic exposition, showing relative-demand curves for labour N_H^d/N_L^d and relative supply of labour N_H^s/N_L^s as a function of relative wage w^h/w^l, where w^h is the wage of high skilled labour and w^l is the wage of low or unskilled labour. Relative demand is defined as demand for (highly) skilled employees (like neurosurgeons or game theorists) relative to low or unskilled employees (like ditch diggers or economic consultants;[1]). The same applies to relative supply.

Figure 1: Relative supply and relative demand

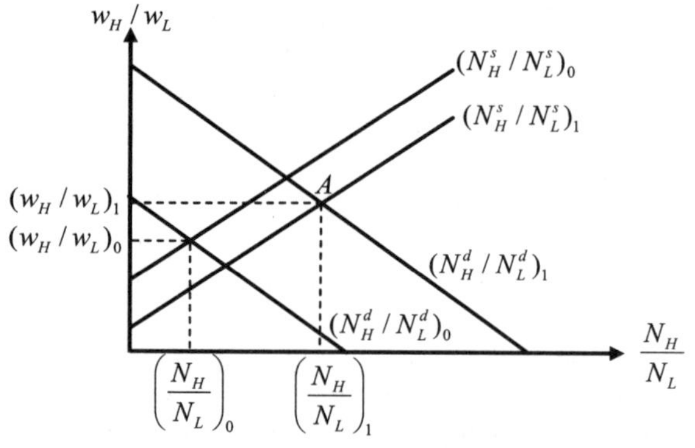

The increase in the relative demand for skilled labour is indicated by the outward shift in the relative-demand curve from $(N_H^d/N_L^d)_0$ to $(N_H^d/N_L^d)_1$. Whether such a shift results in an increase in both relative wage and relative employment depends on whether the relative supply curve (N_H^s/N_L^s) has shifted too. It is very likely that this has indeed been the case in practically all industrialized countries, since the share of people with higher education has been increasing there over the last decades. Depending on the extent to which relative demand and relative supply shift outward, relative wage will either increase or decrease. Since the empirical observation is that both relative employment and relative wages have increased in the last two decades, the shift in the relative supply curve has obviously been overcompensated by the shift in the relative demand curve. In figure 1, this is indicated by point *A*.

It has been argued that an important reason behind this shift was globalization.[2] According to this reasoning, a deeper integration of the world economy leads to a specialization on skill-intensive production in the

---

1 See Johnson, (1997), p. 47.

2 See Borjas / Ramey (1994).

industrialized countries. By contrast, the developing countries would be induced to specialize on non skill-intensive production. However convincing this theoretical reasoning is, it does not seem to fit into empirical findings.[3]

- Trade flows are not big enough to explain these effects.
- The bulk of world trade still takes place among developed countries.
- The industries with the highest increases in world trade have not faced specifically high shifts in relative demand.
- Shifts in relative demand can be observed both in the industrialized as well as in the developing countries.
- Shifts in relative demand can also be observed in industries with no trade.

For these reasons, globalization (alone) is not sufficient for explaining the increase in the wage gap between skilled and unskilled employees in the US and the UK on the one hand and the rising unemployment among unskilled workers in continental Europe.

Most labor-market economists are more convinced in an alternative hypothesis according to which factor enhancing technological progress is the driving force behind the shift in relative demand. The idea is straightforward: Technological change increases productivity of skilled labor and, hence, the demand for high-skilled employees. This hypothesis again appears convincing only at first glance; in this case, however, it is not the empirical facts that contradict its reasoning. Rather, it is the logic behind it which turns out to be a bit trickier than what meets the eye.

2 Technological change, employment and relative wage

Each form of technological change has a specific influence on relative demand for skilled and unskilled labour.[4] Technical change may result in asymmetric productivity shifts across the different industries of an economy. Some industries may face considerable increases in labour productivity, whereas others may only face low increases or no increase at all. In this case we talk about sectoral productivity shifts. So called skill-biased technological change (SBTC) boosts productivity of the skilled workers more than that of the unskilled. Here, so called *extensive* SBTC describes a process during which the skilled workers, together with advanced production routines or robots, substitute unskilled workers.[5] By contrast, one speaks about *intensive* SBTC when productivity of the skilled workers increases on those jobs they have previously already

[3] See Johnson (1997), pp. 46-47; Machin (2003), p. 577.

[4] See Johnson (1997); Haskel (2000).

[5] See Johnson (1997), pp. 47-48.

performed. In this case, productivity of the unskilled employees either remains constant or it increases by a lower rate than that of the skilled workers.

- In the case of intensive SBTC, an increase in relative wages is only plausible when there is no or at least only limited sectoral mobility of employees across the different industries (or sectors). With perfect mobility across the sectors, the relative input of skilled and unskilled labour will change across the different sectors when some sectors produce skill intensive and the others non skill intensive. As a result, relative wages may not change at all.
- With extensive SBTC, whether relative wages rise depends on whether the increase in productivity of the skilled workers lowers unit cost of production, which is not necessarily the case. As far as extensive SBTC does indeed reduce unit costs, its effects are qualitatively identical to those of intensive SBTC. Finally, in the case of sectoral productivity shifts, relative wages will rise if the progress in productivity occurs in the skill-intensive sectors of the economy.
- However, if it occurs in the non skill-intensive sectors, the relative wage will even decrease. Moreover, even if productivity rises in the skill-intensive sector, then this affects relative labour input between skilled and non skilled in a way which contradicts the empirical observations. Namely, production would become less skill intensive in all sectors rather than more skill intensive.

In order to demonstrate these theoretical findings, consider an economy consisting of two sectors, one of which produces skill-intensive whereas the other produces non skill-intensive. Besides skilled and unskilled labour, no further factor of production is employed. Production is called skill intensive if the share of factor income of the skilled employees exceeds 50 percent of total income in the respective sector. A share of less than 50 percent indicates non skill-intensive production. Producers in both sectors face given world-market prices on their output markets. Finally, both sectors produce with constant returns to scale but diminishing marginal productivity of skilled and unskilled labour, respectively.

Due to the duality of cost functions and production functions, a production function can be transformed into a cost function which contains precisely the same information as the corresponding production function.[6] Hence, by assuming profit maximization of all producers and by using *Shephard's* lemma, we can define minimum unit cost functions c^i of the *Cobb-Douglas*-type for each sector:

---

[6] See Shephard (1953); Uzawa (1964).

(1) $$c^i = \left(\frac{w_H^i(N_H^i)}{\alpha_H^i}\right)^{\beta} \cdot \left(\frac{w_L^i(N_L^i)}{\alpha_L^i}\right)^{1-\beta} \qquad \text{with: } i = H, L\ \alpha_H^i, \alpha_L^i > 0;\ 0 \leq \beta \geq 1.$$

Here, $w_H^i(w_L^i)$ is the wage rate of skilled (unskilled) labor as a function of the respective labor input (N_H^i, N_L^i). Finally, α_H^i and α_L^i indicate technological progress which raises productivity of the respective factor of production. Implicit differentiation of (1) yields the following relation between the two wage rates:

(2) $$\frac{dw_H^i}{dw_L^i} = \frac{1-\beta}{\beta} \cdot \frac{w_H^i(N_H^i)}{w_L^i(N_L^i)}.$$

This relation shows the slope of minimum isocost curves between the two wages for skilled and unskilled labour, along each of which unit production costs are constant and at a minimum.[7] The curves are shown as c_{L0}^i and c_{H0}^i in figure 2 for each sector of the economy. By assuming perfect competition, these curves are not only minimum isocost curves but also curves along which profits are zero.

Figure 2: Sectoral shifts versus SBTC

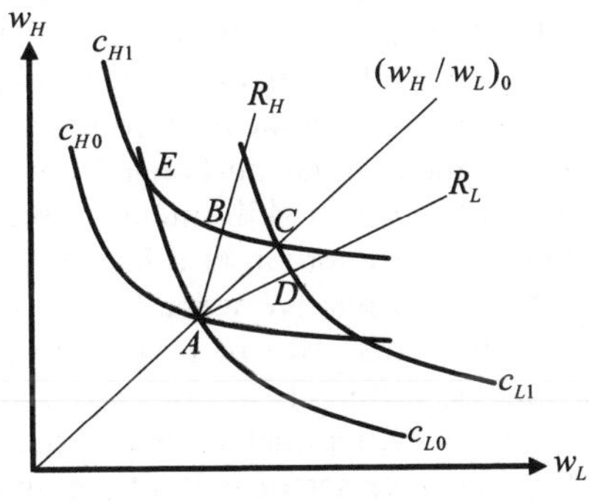

The intersection of the two curves at point A indicates labour-market equilibrium in the economy. The reason is that, with intersectoral mobility of labour, there is but one common wage rate for each type of labour across the sectors. Consider now the budget constraint of the producers in each sector:

(3) $$C^i = w_H^i \cdot N_H + w_L^i \cdot N_L \Leftrightarrow w_H^i = \frac{C^i}{N_H^i} - \frac{N_L^i}{N_H^i} \cdot w_H^i.$$

According to equation (3) the slope of the isocost curves is for every given level of production. Hence, the slope of the respective isocost curve represents relative factor input. Therefore, the steeper isocost curves c_H are those of the non

7 See Woodland (1977).

skill-intensive sector of the economy. Starting from point A in figure 2, the radians R_L and R_H show combinations of w_L and w_H where relative factor input is identical with that in point A. By contrast, all points on the straight line $(w_H/w_L)_0$ indicate a relative wage equal to that in point A. Note that, according to equation (2), the slopes of the curves are independent of α_H^i and α_L^i.

Consider now a sector-neutral SBTC. Sector neutrality implies that $\Delta\alpha_L^L = \Delta\alpha_L^H$ and $\Delta\alpha_H^L = \Delta\alpha_H^H$, whereas SBTC implies $\Delta\alpha_H^i > \Delta\alpha_L^i$. This means that productivity of skilled labour increases at a higher rate than the rate of increase in productivity of unskilled labour, while productivity changes across the sectors are equal. In this case both isocost curves shift proportionally outside along the radians R_L and R_H. A new equilibrium will be found in point C, where the two isocost curves c_{L1} and c_{H1} intersect. Here, the economy wide wage rates of skilled and unskilled labour are proportionally higher than in point *A*, leaving the relative wage rate constant at its initial value $(w_H/w_L)_0$.

The economic rationale behind the move from point *A* to point *C* is as follows.[8] Assume, for a moment, that the two sectors were completely isolated such that there were no flow of labour across the two sectors. Assume further, that each sector would produce with constant relative labour input equal to that in point *A*. The shift of the isocost curves from c_{i0} to c_{i1} would then spread the relative wage rates between the skill-intensive sector and the non skill-intensive sector. The skill intensive sector would move from point *A* to point *B* along the radian R_H, leaving relative labour input unchanged but increasing the relative wage rate w_H/w_L. By contrast, the non skill-intensive sector would move from point *A* to point *D*, which, by assumption, also leaves the relative labour input unchanged but which reduces the relative wage rate. However, in a two-sector economy with mobile labour across two or more sectors, relative wage rates between the sectors cannot be different. In our case, the higher relative wage rate in the skill-intensive sector will attract skilled labour and the lower relative wage rate in the non skill-intensive sector will attract unskilled labour, moving the sectoral labour markets from points *D* and *B* to point *C*. Finally, in Point *C*, the relative wage rate will be equalized across the sectors, but the skill-intensive sector will have a higher relative labour input and the non skill-intensive sector will have a lower relative labour input as compared to any point along the radians R_H and R_L, respectively.

As a result, intensive SBTC will deepen the specialization between skill-intensive production and non skill-intensive production. It can, however, neither explain a general increase in relative employment of skilled employees, nor can it explain an increase in the relative wage rate of the skilled employees. In order to explain an increase in the relative wage rate, one could assume some sectoral

---

[8] See Haskel (2000); Jones (2000).

technological change.[9] In an extreme case, technological progress would only occur in one sector, say the skill-intensive sector. This would shift the isocost curve of the skill-intensive sector from c_{H0} to c_{H1} in figure 2, but would leave the isocost curve of the non skill-intensive sector unchanged at c_{L0}. The new equilibrium would be at point *E*. The economic rationale behind this new equilibrium can again be understood by assuming, for a moment, isolated sectors and constant relative labour input. In this case, the skill-intensive sector would move from point *A* to point *B*, whereas the non skill-intensive sector would stick with point *A*. Note that in point *B*, wage rates of both skilled and unskilled labour are higher than in point *A*. Hence, skilled and unskilled labour would be induced to move from the non skill-intensive sector to the skill intensive sector. However, a relatively high share of those who move to the skill-intensive sector is unskilled, whereas production in that sector requires a relatively high share of skilled employees. This raises relative scarcity of the skilled as compared to the unskilled employees. As a consequence, the relative wage rate of the skilled employees rises.

From the point of view of the economy as a whole, sectoral technology changes which raise labour productivity in the skill-intensive sector, lead to an increase in relative scarcity of skilled labour. This raises the relative wage rate of skilled labor. At the same time, it induces a substitution of scarce skilled labour by the less scarce unskilled labour. In equilibrium (point *E*), relative wage of skilled labour is higher but relative employment of skilled labour is lower than before the technology shift occurred.

Summing up, neither intensive SBTC nor sectoral technology shifts alone can explain the empirical observation of an increase in the relative wage rate and, at the same time, an increase in relative employment of skilled labour. A satisfactory explanation of this development requires some further aspects to be taken in consideration as well. For example, repercussions from the world market of the *Stolper-Samuelson*-type have been analyzed.[10] If there is an increase in skill input on a broad basis all over the world, then world-wide supply of manufactured products and, thus, world-market prices tend to fall. The effects on relative wages and relative labour input, however, will be similar to those of the productivity shifts. Hence it remains to be clarified what the driving factors behind the increase in relative wages and relative employment over the last two decades have been. Whatever these driving forces behind the shifts in relative labour demand have been, continental European labour markets have reacted quite differently on these shifts as compared to those in the United States and Great Britain. Whereas the latter saw increases in employment and a rising

---

[9] See Dluhosch (2003).

[10] See Dluhosch (2003), pp. 171-174.

spread in wages, continental Europe still faces increasing unemployment especially among the low or non skilled people. The next section tries to explain why this has been so.

3 Labour-market rigidities and technology shifts

For the sake of simplicity, let us switch back to a single-sector economy in order to look at the effects of labour-market rigidities with shifts in the structure of labour demand. Look at figure 3 for an exposition of a simple dual labour-market model.[11] For reasons of simplicity, labour supply is considered as exogenous and inelastic with respect to the wage rate. Read from the left to the right, the graph in figure 3 depicts input of skilled persons N_H. Read from the right, input of non skilled employees is depicted as N_L. Accordingly, the lines N^d_{H0} and N^d_{L0} represent labour demand. Since we assume competitive markets, these lines also represent the slope of marginal productivity for both types of labour. In equilibrium, there will be an equal wage rate $w_{H0}=w_{L0}$ for both qualification. The initial allocation of labour will be N_{H0}, N_{L0}. For the sake of simplicity we abstract from costs of investment in human capital. Hence, there is no premium on the wage rate which compensates for former human capital investment of any employee.

Figure 3: Short- and long-term scenario in a dual labour market

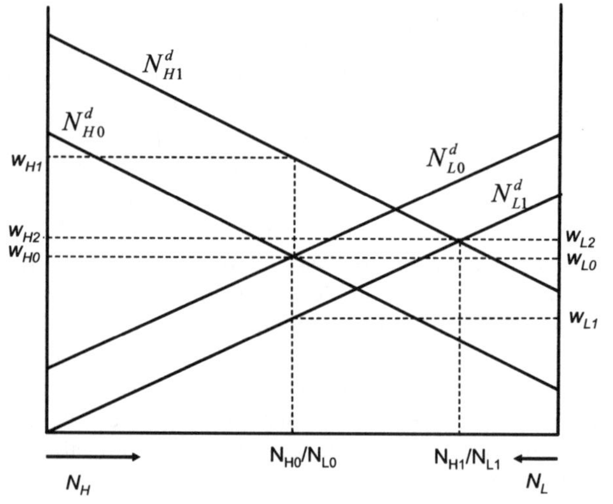

Suppose now the structure of demand for labour changes. Demand for high-skilled labour increases, shifting the demand curve outwards from N^d_{H0} to N^d_{H1}. At

[11] See Burda / Dluhosch (1999); Jones (1987); Christensen (2001); Prinz (2004).

the same time, demand for low-skilled labour drops, shifting the demand curve from N^d_{L0} to N^d_{L1}. We can now distinguish three different scenarios. In the first scenario there are flexible wages but immobile labour across the qualifications, i.e. employees cannot switch from low skilled to high skilled supply. Let us call that the short-term scenario. In this scenario, the wage rate of the unskilled employees drops to a level of w_{L1}, whereas the wage rate of the skilled employyees increases to w_{H1}. The resulting spread in the wage structure leaves the allocation of labour unchanged but nevertheless clears both labour market segments.

In the second scenario there are both flexible wages and mobility of labour supply across the two qualifications. Let us call this the long-term scenario since it takes time for the suppliers of labour to switch from supply of unskilled to supply of skilled labour. In the long-term scenario the higher wage rate for skilled labour induces employees to shift from supplying non skilled to supplying skilled labour. Since we abstract from costs of building human capital, the employees will shift their labour supply until the wage rates in the two sectors are equalized at $w_{H2} = w_{L2}$. The new equilibrium will be associated with a reallocation of labour to N_{H1}/N_{L1}, i.e. more skilled workers and less unskilled workers will be employed. Again, the labour market will be cleared.

Figure 4: Rigid wages and immobility across qualifications in a dual labour market

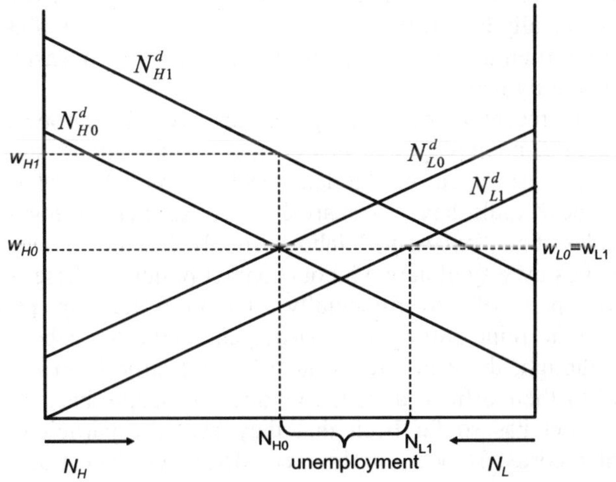

Finally, let us turn to the third scenario, which we may call the Continental-European scenario. In this scenario wages are rigid and there is no labour mobility across the qualifications. More precisely, wages are inflexible in the downward direction. The implications are shown in figure 4. The wage rate for skilled labour increases to w_{H1} whereas the wage rate for unskilled labour remains constant. Employment of the non skilled drops from N_{L0} to N_{L1}. As a result, there will be a shortage of skilled labour and, at the same time, structural unemployment to the extent of N_{H0}-N_{L1} for the unskilled. Hence, employment of skilled labour will fall short of what it would be in the case of mobility across the qualifications. In sum, employment will decrease.

There is plenty of evidence that the wage structure in continental Europe is indeed much more rigid than in the US or in the UK. However, it is not quite clear why there is also a greater extent of immobility of labour supply across the qualifications in continental Europe, as compared to the US and the UK. The reasons are manifold. One reason is wage rigidity itself. With rigid wages, structural shifts in labour demand will imply a less pronounced spread in the wage rates, which lowers incentives for investment in human capital. True, if the wage spread is not sufficiently high in order to restore market clearing in both sectors unemployment will result, which induces people to switch as well. However, this mechanism has also been hampered in continental Europe, and especially in Germany, for a number of reasons. These reasons are, *inter alia*, regulations regarding legal requirements and formal qualifications for employees who apply for specific jobs; a dysfunctional so called "active labour-market policy" that aims at qualifying employees but, in practice, merely keeps employees in training programs and out of the unemployment statistics; unemployment and welfare benefits which are not only generous but are also granted for unusually long time periods; and an extensive use of early-retirement schemes. More often than not, the result from such policy measures is persistent structural unemployment.

At least until recently, the public-policy approach in Europe to mitigate the ensuing structural unemployment has been to reduce labour supply. The most important tools are open or hidden mechanisms that reduce the age of retirement. These tools have extensively been applied during the 1980s and 1990s. Besides that, "excessive" labour supply has been removed from the official statistics by way of active labour-market policies. These policies consist, for the most part, of governmentally monitored training programs which officially aim at reintegrating the participants into the labour market. Unfortunately, though, these programs have by and large been rather ineffective with respect to their official aim, i.e. getting the people back on jobs. Rather, their main effect has so far been that they kept the participants off the unemployment records. Hence, employment decreased. The tragic of the story, however, is that the unemployment rate increased nevertheless. Admittedly, this is not true for each country in continental Europe. For example, Denmark and The Netherlands have, at least at times, been pretty successful in bringing people back on jobs via properly designed training programs. This, however, does not apply to other countries, namely not for Germany and Italy.

Let us push our considerations a little further in order to explain why the unemployment rate rose despite of the reduction in labour supply.[12] To start with, consider a linear-homogenous production function of a representative firm with the usual properties:

(4) $X(N,K)$ with: $X_N > 0; X_K > 0; X_{NN} < 0; X_{KK} < 0; X_{NK} > 0; X_{KN} > 0,$

with subscripts indicating partial derivatives. There are two inputs, namely unskilled labour (*N*) and capital (*K*). Assume now the following simple profit function of a representative firm:

(5) $\text{Pr} = P \cdot X(N, K) - w \cdot N - P_K \cdot K.$

Here Pr is profit, *P* the price on a competitive goods market and P_K a supply price of capital on a perfect capital market. A profit maximizing labour input would then suffice the usual first-order condition:

(6) $X_N = \frac{w}{P}.$

Note that, because of the assumptions made in (4), the position of the demand curve for labour in a wage-labour space depends on the amount of capital invested. Specifically, a rising capital stock shifts the labour-demand curve outwards and *vice versa*. Let us now define the production per employee as $x \equiv X/N$ and the capital intensity as $k \equiv K/N$. We can then rewrite the profit function (5) as:

(7) $\text{Pr} = P \cdot x(k) \cdot N - w \cdot N - P_K \cdot k \cdot N.$

The first-order condition with respect to the profit-maximizing capital intensity k^* is:

(8) $x_k(k^*) = \frac{P_K}{P}.$

In addition to the condition (6) for an optimal labour input, a profit maximum also requires that, according to condition (8), the marginal return of an increase in the capital intensity equals the real supply price of capital. Hence, given the properties of the underlying production function, there is but one capital intensity k^* which is compatible with a profit maximum. Now look at figure 5. The initial equilibrium can be found in the upper part of the figure as the intersection of the demand curve N_0^d and the inelastic supply curve N_0^s. Employment in this initial situation is as high as N_f, and there is no unemployment. At the same time, the optimal capital intensity k^* is realized, as can be seen in the lower part of figure 5. The straight line k^* through the origin

---

[12] See Hamermesh (1986).

represents all combinations of labour input N and capital input K that are associated with an optimal capital intensity k^*. In the initial equilibrium, labour input N_f is combined with the capital input K_f. Hence, a point on the k^*-line is realized.

Consider now a decrease in the demand for unskilled labour. The demand curve then shifts inwards from N_0^d to N_1^d. With flexible wages, the wage rate would drop to the new market-clearing level w_e. With rigid wages, however, the wage rate remains constant, resulting in unemployment to the extent of u_0. Assume that, in order to remove the unemployed persons from the unemployment statistics, government reduces labour supply to a level of N_0. Employment will then remain low, but the official unemployment rate will be reduced to zero. This, however, cannot be a stable equilibrium. The reason is that the reduced level of employment from N_f to N_0 increases the capital intensity, as can be seen in the lower part of figure 5. As long as the representative firm has not yet adjusted its capital stock, point A will be realized, associated with a capital intensity of k^t. Since this capital intensity violates condition (4) for the profit-maximizing capital intensity, the firm will restore the profit maximum by reducing its capital stock from K_f to K_0.

***Figure 5*:** The reappearance of unemployment

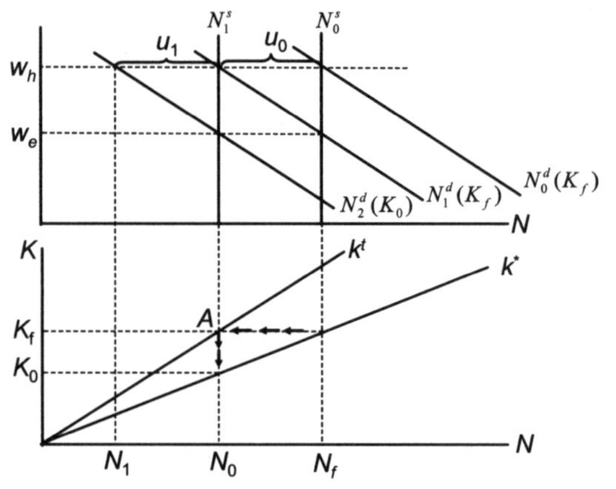

This reduction, in turn, will affect the demand function for labour in the upper part of the graph, since the demand function is equal to marginal productivity of labour X_N and, by the assumption of equation (4), $X_{NK} > 0$. Hence a decrease in the capital stock will shift the demand curve for labour further inwards to N_2^d. Unemployment to the extent of u_2 will result. No matter how hard a government tries to hide unemployment by reducing labour supply, it will always reappear as soon as the firms adjust their capital stock to the lower level of employment. What is worse, this vicious circle of increasing unemployment, decreasing employment and disinvestment will continue in ever new rounds unless wages move to the market-clearing level w_e.

4 Concluding remarks

No matter what the reasons behind the shifts in the demand structure for labour over the last two decades have been, the large continental European Countries have been poor at coping with the challenges implied in these shifts. Rigid labour markets have prevented market forces from equilibrating supply and demand for skilled and unskilled labour, and public policy has failed to develop proper measures in order to improve the labour markets' capacities for restoring equilibrium. What is worse, the defensive strategy of removing excess labour supply, specifically that of low or falsely qualified persons, from the labour market, has left behind a disastrous heritage. It reduced unemployment only temporarily, and it reduced employment from the very beginning, driving state budgets and social security funds in ever deeper deficits, long before the future demographic problems materialize. Hopefully, after more than two decades of a failed labour-market policy, we will eventually be able to switch to a more promising strategy; a strategy that relies on market forces, even on the labour market.

Literature

Borjas, G. J; V. Ramey (1994): Time Series Evidence on the Sources of Trends in Wage Inequality, in: American Economic Review 84, pp. 10-16.

Burda, M.; B. Dluhosch (1999): Globalization and European Labor Markets, in: Globalization and Labor, Tübingen: Mohr, pp. 181-207.

Christensen, B. (2001): Qualifikationsanforderungen und Arbeitsformen in der Neuen Ökonomie, in: Institute for World Economy Working Paper Series, Working Paper No. 1081/2001, Kiel.

Dluhosch, B. (2003): Humankapitalmangel in der New Economy?, in: Schäfer, W. (ed.), Konjunktur, Wachstum und Wirtschaftspolitik im Zeichen der New Economy, Berlin: Duncker & Humblot, pp. 157-181.

Hamermesh, D. S. (1986): The Demand for Labor in the Long Run, in: Ashenfelter, O. and Layard, R. (eds.), Handbook of Labor Economics, Vol. 1, Amsterdam: North-Holland, pp. 429-471.

Haskel, J. E. (2000): Trade and Labor Approaches to Wage Inequality, in: Review of International Economics 8, pp. 397-408.

Johnson, G. E. (1997): Changes in Earnings Inequality: The Role of Demand Shifts, in: Journal of Economic Perspectives 11, pp. 41-54.

Jones, S. R. G. (1987): Minimum Wage Legislation in a Dual Labor Market, in: European Economic Review 31, pp. 1229-1246.

Jones, R. W. (2000): Technical Progress, Price Adjustments, and Wages, in: Review of International Economics 8, pp. 497-503.

Machin, S. (2003): Skill-Biased Technical Change in the New Economy, in: Jones, D. C. (ed.), New Economy Handbook, Amsterdam: Elsevier, pp. 565-581.

Prinz, A. (2004): Reform der Arbeitsmarktpolitik. Alter Wein in alten Schläuchen?, in: Perspektiven der Wirtschaftspolitik 4, pp. 313-332.

Shephard, R. W. (1953): Cost and Production Functions, Princeton: Princeton University Press.

Uzawa, H. (1964): Duality Principles in the Theory of Cost and Production, in: International Economic Review 5, pp. 216-220.

Woodland, A. D. (1977): A Dual Approach to Equilibrium in the Production Sector in International Trade Theory, in: Canadian Journal of Economics 10, pp. 50-68.

International trade and employment: A sectoral and regional analysis for Germany and the EU25

by

Gustav Dieckheuer

1 Background and questions

Most countries in the former EU-15 are renowned for their remarkable export strength. But for many years this has been matched by moderate GDP growth and persistent high unemployment levels. Obviously, the economic impulses of increased exports on the domestic economies are comparatively weak. This is caused by high growth rates of labour productivities as well as increasing import intensities, especially in the export sectors. Both of these facts give an explanation for the small impulses from exports on the domestic labour markets and on national income. These developments are comparatively strong in Germany's main export sectors like automobile and machine industries. Therefore it is not astonishing that on the one hand Germany is export champion worldwide but on the other hand the country suffers from persistent high unemployment and comparatively low GDP-growth rates.[1]

Figure 1: Export-employment ratios in the EU-25 (1995 – 100)

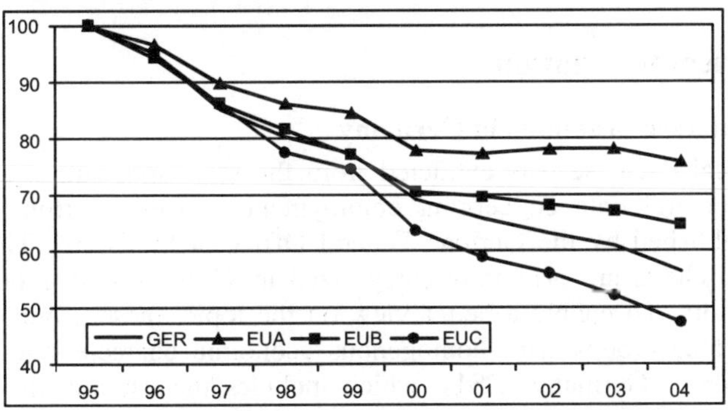

Figure 1 gives an impression of the diminishing role of exports for employment in the EU-25. In Germany the macroeconomic ratio of exports to employment

---

[1] At present there is an intensive discussion about the importance of exports for the German economy and related developments of employment and value added in Germany, for example: Brautzsch / Ludwig (2004), (2005); Clement / Natrop (2004); Dieckheuer (2004); Horn / Behncke (2004); Flassbeck, H. (2004), IWD (2003), Schintke, J. und Weiß, J.P. (2003), Schneider, St. (2004), Sinn (2005).

between 1995 and 2004 decreased by nearly 45%. The decline of this ratio was remarkably lower in EU-country group EUA (Great Britain, France, Italy and Netherlands) and in the rest of the former EU-15 (EUB), but it was higher in the new EU-member countries. However, the result for the new members was highly influenced by the transition process, and it is to be expected that the sharp decline of the export-employment ratio will be damped sooner or later.

The above mentioned situation gives the impetus for a broader analysis of national intersectoral links in Germany and of export-import links within the EU-25. On a theoretical and empirical basis a national input-output-model for Germany and an international export-import-model for country-groups of the EU-25 will be constructed to investigate the following questions:

- In which way do sector-specific changes in German exports affect GDP and employment in Germany as well as in other EU-countries and how did these effects develop since 1995?
- How important is the outsourcing of parts of the value added chain to other national sectors on the one hand and to other EU-countries on the other hand for the GDP and employment effects of additional German exports?
- How will the value added and employment effects of additional German exports be distributed among the different sectors in Germany?
- How will the GDP and employment effects of additional German exports be distributed among the EU countries?

2 Empirical foundations

2.1 The intersectoral links in Germany

The empirical database was extracted from the real input-output-calculations, from the sectoral data concerning employment as well as from the import matrices published by the German Federal Office of Statistics.[2] The available input-output-charts are originally categorized in 71 groups of goods and production sectors. To enable a better view on the topic, these groups have been merged to four groups with homogenous economic characteristics: the main export sector of Germany **(ES1)**, which includes the car and the machinery industries, the other important export sector **(ES2)**, especially chemistry, metal, textile and food industries, the firm related service sectors **(FRS)**, which include services in the field of research and development, and the other sectors **(REST)** comprising mainly services like banks, insurances, transport, commerce, health care and public services.

Input-output-tables with reliable data are currently only available up to the year 2000. However, at the time of this study all macroeconomic data and a lot

[2] Statistisches Bundesamt (2002), (2004).

of sectoral data including those of 2004 were available. By using this data the input-output-tables following the year 2000 were extrapolated. Nevertheless, the input-coefficients had to be calculated by trend procedures. Therefore, the intersectoral links for the years 2001 to 2004 are somewhat uncertain. But, based on compatibility tests relating to the available data, one can draw the conclusion that the differences between estimation and reality should not be serious. For that reason the results of the simulation are indeed meaningful.

Table 1 shows the input-output table of Germany for the year 2004. The export sectors ES1 and ES2 together had a proportion of 70% of total German exports in 2004. Direct imports represent a relative high share of 16% in exports, and merely 14% account for the remaining sectors FRS and REST. The export sectors' share in total German production was about one third, but their contribution to the total value added and to employment amounts to just 20%.

Table 1: Input-output-table for Germany 2004 (€ bn in prices of 1995; employment in million employees)

to / from	ES1	ES2	FRS	REST	DA	EX	Σ
ES1	117.54	8.75	1.40	33.47	120.02	318.76	599.94
ES2	60.77	111.01	4.72	85.01	159.99	232.65	654.15
FRS	43.93	48.96	43.13	135.74	50.30	23.11	345.17
REST	70.73	138.35	42.34	553.58	1,250.76	104.49	2,160.25
IM	131.68	129.50	17.02	105.07	180.64	125.78	689.69
TS	2.20	1.43	1.70	35.22	140.23	-0.94	
VA	173.09	216.15	234.86	1,212.16	–	–	
Σ	599.94	654.15	345.17	2,160.25	1,901.94	803.85	
E	3.31	4.44	4.52	26.17			

Sectors: ES1: main export sectors; ES2: other important export sectors; FRS: firm related services; REST: all other sectors.
Sectoral and macroeconomic data: DA: Domestic absorption; EX: Exports; IM: Imports; TS: Indirect taxes minus subsidies; VA: Value added; E: Employment.

2.2 Export-import-links in the EU-25

The importance of an economic sector for GDP, value added and employment can only be grasped completely if the international export-import-linkages are also taken into account. Indeed, some branches have removed parts of their value-added chain to foreign countries and therefore enlarged their import quota in the domestic production process, but the production of those intermediate inputs has a positive influence on employment and income abroad, which usually induces further exports from Germany to foreign countries. The currently available data enable us only to identify the linkages and effects for the EU-25. The data about trade linkages of Germany and the other EU-25 countries with countries outside the EU are still too incomplete to gain an accurate insight into the interdependencies and resulting effects. For this reason only the linkages within the EU-25 are recorded endogenously in the further analysis.

EU-countries besides Germany are split into three groups: group **EUA** contains the main trade partners of Germany (Great Britain, France, Italy and the Netherlands); group **EUB** includes the rest of the members of the former EU-15 (Belgium, Denmark, Finland, Greece, Ireland, Luxemburg, Austria, Portugal, Sweden, Spain); the third group **EUC** consists of the new EU-accession countries (Estonia, Latvia, Lithuania, Malta, Poland, Slovakia, Slovenia, Czech Republic, Hungary, Cyprus). All remaining countries of the world are summed up in the group **RW**. For the EU-25-members data of the macroeconomic parameters up to 2004 are available. In contrast, data of import coefficients of the trade between the EU-countries are available only up to 2002. Therefore, export-import tables for the years 2003 and 2004 could only be extrapolated by trend calculations of the missing coefficients. Although this implies uncertainty, compatibility tests again come to the conclusion that the used data are close to reality.

Table 2 shows the data for the year 2004. The grey area contains the trade linkages between Germany and the three country groups of the remaining EU-25. According to these data Germany exported goods of € 232.17 bn to EUA, € 164.97 bn to the group EUB and € 45.15 bn to the new EU-countries (group EUC). With regard to the same groups of countries the import value was € 219.90 bn, € 147.36 bn and € 73.92 bn. The exports and imports of the EU-member-groups with Germany and among each other can be read accordingly. In addition, the exports from and imports to the rest of the world are displayed for Germany and the three EU-country-groups.

The table finally contains data of the domestic absorption (consumption and investment) in Germany as well as in the three country-groups of the EU-25, of the final demand FD (sum of domestic absorption and exports), of the gross domestic product GDP (final demand minus imports) and data concerning employment E (measured in millions of employees).

Table 2: Export-import-table for the EU-25 in 2004 (bn € in prices of 1995; employment in million employees)

to / from	GER	EUA	EUB	EUC	RW	EX	DA	FD
GER	—	232.17	164.96	45.15	361.59	803.86	1,901.93	2,705.79
EUA	219.90	285.40	299.12	33.41	490.41	1,328.24	3,963.94	5,292.18
EUB	147.36	272.04	146.18	25.18	398.31	989.06	1,887.36	2,876.42
EUC	73.92	36.07	36.56	21.27	39.89	207.71	334.80	542.51
RW	248.51	575.20	266.19	94.50				
IM	689.69	1,400.87	913.00	219.50				
Y	2,016.10	3,891.31	1,963.42	323.01				
FD	2,705.79	5,292.18	2,876.42	542.51				
E	**38.27**	**84.83**	**45.69**	**30.35**				

Countries: GER: Germany; EUA: Main trade partners of Germany within the EU-25 (France, Great Britain, Italy, Netherlands); EUB: Remaining countries of former EU-15 (Austria, Belgium, Denmark, Finland, Greece, Ireland, Luxemburg, Portugal, Spain, Sweden); EUC: New members of EU (Cyprus, Estonia, Hungary, Latvia, Lithuania, Malta, Poland, Slovakia, Slovenia, Czech Republic); RW: Rest of the world.

Data: E: Employment; Y: Gross national product; DA: Domestic absorption; FD: Final demand.

Source: Eurostat (2005); International Monetary Fund (2005); Statistisches Bundesamt (2005a), (2005b); own calculations.

The grey area of the export-import-matrix contains the by far greatest part of the international transactions of the countries within the EU-25. The export and import quotas displayed in figure 2 are received from this table. Therefore, the countries of the EU-25 originate a share of 55% in the total German exports in 2004, and 64% of the German imports derive from these countries. The EU-25-countries sell 18% of their exports to Germany, and further 46% are obtained through intraregional trade within the EU. On the import side the figures are almost the same (17% and respectively 46%). It becomes apparent that on the one hand Germany has the highest export quota within the EU-25, but on the other hand its exports to the rest of the world (about 45%) were relatively high, too. Since 1995 this proportion has been increasing permanently (in 1995 it added up to solely about 35%). Obviously, Germany has succeeded in opening up new markets in countries outside the EU faster than other EU-countries did.

Figure 2: Export and import quota within the EU-25 in 2004

a) Export and import quota of Germany's trade with EU-25	b) Export and import quota of EU-25-countries trade with Germany

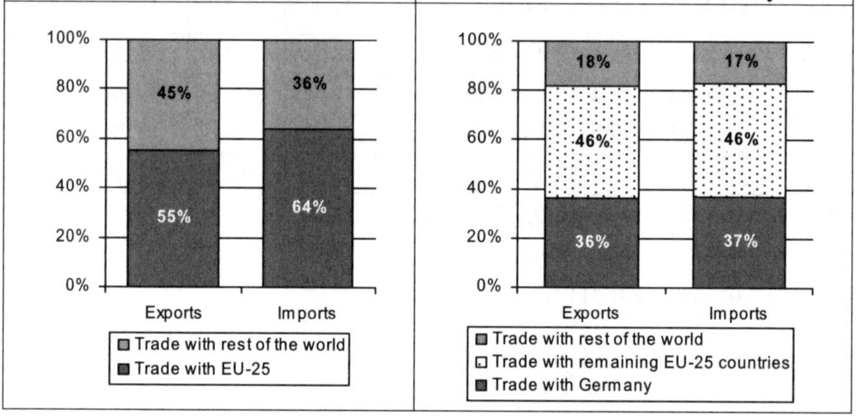

3 Theoretical foundations

3.1 The national input-output-model

The following analysis is based on an input-output-model to explain intersectoral and macroeconomic linkages within Germany.[3] Table 3 gives a review of the underlying input-output structure.

With reference to the variables displayed in the table the model consists of the following equations, whereas the symbols i and j represent the four different sectors in the analysis. For the output value X_j of a sector j the following applies:

(1) $$X_j = \Sigma b_{ij} Z_i + DA_j + EX_j \qquad \text{with } j = 1, 2, ...i, ...n$$

The output value of sector j on the one hand consists of the intermediate inputs to the sectors i (including sector j) and on the other hand of the final demand for products of this sector. Intermediate input demand of the sectors i in the sector j arises from the product of the input coefficient b_{ij} and the whole domestic intermediate input demand Z_i of the sectors i. Attention should be paid to the fact that input coefficients in the applied model relate to the demand for intermediate inputs from domestic production and not to the sectors' output values. Final demand consists of domestic absorption DA and exports EX.

---

3 For Input-output-analysis: Schumann (1968); Miller / Blair (1985); Leontief (1987); Holub / Schnabl (1997). For an intersectoral model: Dieckheuer (2004), (2005).

Domestic absorption includes private and governmental consumption and investment demand. The sectoral domestic absorption DA_j of a sector j is part of the total domestic absorption DA and will be explained by means of the sector specific absorption coefficient h_j. These absorption-coefficients are either calculated from the annual input-output-tables or in case of yet missing data (2001 up to 2004) by trend calculations.

(2) $DA_j = h_j DA$ with $j = 1, 2, \ldots i, \ldots n$

Table 3: Input-output-structure of the model

		Sectoral input				Final Demand		Sum
		1	i	•	n	DA	EX	
Sectoral output	1	$b_{11}Z_1$	$b_{i1}Z_i$	•	$b_{n1}Z_n$	DA_1	EX_1	X_1
	j	$b_{1i}Z_1$	$b_{ij}Z_j$	•	$b_{ni}Z_n$	DA_j	EX_j	X_j
	•	•	•	•	•	•	•	•
	n	$b_{1n}Z_1$	$b_{in}Z_i$	•	$b_{nn}Z_n$	DA_n	EX_n	X_n
Domestic intermediate goods		Z_1	Z_i	•	Z_n	–	–	–
Imported goods (IM)		IM_1	IM_i	•	IM_n	IM_{DA}	IM_{EX}	**IM_G**
Total intermediate goods		V_1	V_i	•	V_n	–	–	
Indirect taxes minus subsidies		TS_1	TS_i	•	TS_n	TS_{DA}	TS_{EX}	
Value added (VA)		VA_1	VA_i	•	VA_n	–	–	
Sum		X_1	X_i	•	X_n	**DA_G**	**EX_G**	
Employment (E)		E_1	E_i	•	E_n			

Symbols: E: Employment (amount of employees); EX: Exports; DA: Domestic absorption; IM: Imports; b: Input coefficient of domestic intermediate inputs; i and j: Sectors.

The exports EX_j of a sector j are composed of autonomous exports, which are exogenously given, and induced exports, which are explained endogenously. The induced exports result from the product of the sectoral export coefficients e_j and the total exports EX_G of a country, in this case Germany (symbol G). The export coefficients are known from the annual input-output-tables or in case of missing data (2001 up to 2004) calculated by trend calculations. Therefore, the sectoral export function sums up to:

(3) $EX_j = EXA_j + e_j EX_G$ with $j = 1,2, \ldots i, \ldots n$

The intermediate input of a sector i from domestic production results as follows:

(4) $Z_i = (1 - m_i)V_i$

V_i describes the total intermediate input used by the sector i; m_i is the input coefficient of this sectors' imported intermediate goods. The total amount of intermediate input of a sector i results from a linear relationship with this sectors' output value.

(5) $V_i = v_i X_i$

The total value added VA_i of a sector i corresponds with the difference between output value X_i, total intermediate input V_i and the difference TS_j between the taxes on goods and the received governmental subsidies of this sector. Using the sectoral tax-subsidies-quota g_i the parameter TS_i is explained in linear relationship with the output value X_i.

(6) $VA_i = X_i - V_i - TS_i = (1 - g_i)X_i - V_i$

The employment in a sector i (measured by the number of employees in this sector) results from the ratio of output value X_i and the sector's productivity (related to the employment) a_i.

(7) $E_i = \frac{1}{a_i} X_i$

The total domestic absorption DA consists of private consumer demand C, private investment demand I and final demand of the state DA_s. C and I each are explained in relation to the total value added VA, whereas DA_s is an exogenous figure.

(8) $DA = C + I + DA_s$

The private marginal quota of consumption (related to the total value added) was estimated for the years 1995 to 2004, using data from the German Federal Office of Statistics.

(9) $C = C^a + C(VA) = 101.49 + 0.5699 \cdot VA$ $R^2 = 0.9532$

Private investment demand is compounded of investment in plant and equipment and inventory investment. Concerning the first, annual investment quotas β were acquired from the available national accounting data of the years 1995 to 2004. Furthermore, they were adjusted via trend procedures up to the year 2004. The inventory investment is an autonomous variable.

(10) $I = I^a + \beta \cdot VA$

The total value added in the economy VA is the sum of the total values added VA_i of all sectors i:

(11) $VA = \Sigma VA_i$

The total imports IM contain the sum of the sectors' i imported intermediate inputs and the direct imports included in the domestic absorption IM_{DA} as well as the exports IM_{EX}. The imported intermediate inputs are the product of the sector specific import quota m_i and the intermediate inputs V_i of a sector i. Accordingly, direct imports are explained with the help of the import quotas m_{DA} und m_{EX} in dependence on total domestic absorption DA and total exports EX respectively. Therefore, the following applies:

$$IM = \Sigma m_i V_i + IM_{DA} + IM_{EX} = \Sigma m_i V_i + m_{DA} DA + m_{EX} EX \quad (12)$$

3.2 The international export-import-model

The input-output-model outlined above exclusively considers Germany. Through the therein contained exports and imports, linkages to the other countries of the EU-25 as well as to the rest of the world were established (Table 4). The EU-25 is divided into the single country Germany (Index G) and the groups k or q (up to n), each representing several countries. Furthermore, all countries outside the EU-25 are consolidated in the group "rest of the world" (index R). There also exist export-import-links within a group of countries of the EU-25.

Table 4: Export-import-structure of the model

		Exports to EU-25-countries or groups of countries				Exports to the rest of the world	Final demand		
		G	k	•	n		Σ (EX)	DA	Σ (FD)
Imports from EU-25-countries	G	–	$d_{kG}IM_k$	•	$d_{nG}IM_n$	EX_{RG}	$\mathbf{EX_G}$	$\mathbf{DA_G}$	$\mathbf{FD_G}$
	q	$d_{Gq}IM_G$	$d_{kq}M_k$	•	$d_{nq}IM_n$	EX_{Rq}	EX_q	DA_q	FD_q
	•	•	•	•	•	•	•	•	•
	n	$d_{Gn}IM_G$	$d_{kn}IM_k$	•	$d_{nn}IM_n$	EX_{Rn}	EX_n	DA_n	FD_n
Imports from the rest of the world		$d_{GR}IM_G$	$d_{kR}IM_k$	•	$d_{nR}IM_n$				
Total imports (IM)		$\mathbf{IM_G}$	IM_k	•	IM_n				
Gross domestic product (Y)		Y_G	Y_k	•	Y_n				
Final demand (FD)		EN_G	EN_k	•	EN_n				
Employment (E)		$\mathbf{BE_G}$	$\mathbf{BE_k}$	•	$\mathbf{BE_n}$				

Symbols: E: Employment (number of employees); G: Symbol for Germany; FD: Final demand; EX: Exports; DA: Domestic absorption; IM: Imports; Y: Gross domestic product; d: Import coefficient; k, q to n: sectors.

Germany's total exports consist of exports to the other countries of the EU-25 and exports to the rest of the world. Exports to the other EU-25-countries are equal to their imports from Germany. In the model, these imports are determined endogenously. In fact, as a product of import coefficient d_{kG} and the total imports IM_k of the country group k:

(13) $EX_G = \Sigma EX_k + EX_{RG} = \Sigma d_{kG} IM_k + EX_{RG}$

The total exports of a country group q (= k) result accordingly, whereas:

(14) $EX_q = EX_{Gq} + \Sigma d_{kq} IM_k + EX_{Rq}$

In the model, the exports EX_{RG} and EX_{Rq} to the rest of the world are exogenously given.

The imports of the country group k are endogenously explained.[4] They result by considering the import quota m_k in relation to the country group's gross national product Y_k:

(15) $IM_k = m_k Y_k$

This equation applies accordingly for Germany:

(16) $IM_G = m_G Y_G$

The gross national product of this country group k responds ex definitione to the difference between final demand on products and the imports of the considered country group:

(17) $Y_k = FD_k - IM_k$

This applies for Germany as well:

(18) $Y_G = FD_G - IM_G$

A country group's final demand q (= k) contains exports EX_q and domestic absorption DA_q:

(19) $FD_q = EX_q + DA_q$

Again, this applies to Germany analogously. Of course, Germany's final demand is already contained in the national input-output-table 4:

---

[4] From the estimations and calculations it follows that the average import quota of the EU-25-countries without Germany has risen significantly between 1995 and 2004, namely from 0.299 in 1995 successively to 0.41 in 2004. In contrast, the portion of imports from Germany related to total imports of these countries have declined from 0.192 in 1995 to 0.174 in 2004. Compared to this, the German import quota has increased from 0.238 in 1995 to 0.342 in 2004. The share in imports from other EU-countries has slightly decreased from about 0.66 in 1995 to 0.64 in the year 2004.

(20) $FD_G = EX_G + DA_G$

Germany's domestic absorption has already been defined in equation (8). The domestic absorption of a country group is also endogenously calculated, in this case in dependence on the gross national product Y_q of this country group. The marginal quota of domestic absorption is derived for the years 1995 to 2004 by estimating private quota of consumption and marginal quota of investment with the help of the available data. The autonomous domestic absorption DA_q^a was acquired as a residual. In the model, it is considered as exogenously given.[5]

In general, the function sums up to:

(21) $DA_q = DA_q^a + h_q Y_q$

Finally, the employment E_k in the country group k has to be explained endogenously. In contrast to the case of Germany according to equation (7), a relationship to the country group's gross national product Y_k is established with the help of the productivity a_k. This distinction is necessary because for the other countries of the EU-25 no intersectoral linkages are available and therefore the sectoral output values are unknown. Henceforth, the following applies:

(22) $E_k = \frac{1}{a_k} Y_k$

4 Sectoral effects[6]

4.1 Intrasectoral effects

In the following section, it is examined which effects on employment, value added and intermediate inputs occur within a sector if this sector's exports rise. Alternatively, an autonomous increase of the exports by the main export sectors ES1 and by the furthermore important export sector ES2 is modelled. In each period exports are increased by the identical amount of €1 bn. That means they are €1 bn higher than the basic value in each period. The raise in exports is caused by an autonomous increase in demand of the countries outside the EU-25. By this it is guaranteed that the increase in final demand is exclusively

---

5 For the average marginal quota of consumption of the EU-25 without Germany a value of 0.544 arises from the estimation. The average quota of investment has successively risen from 0.189 in 1995 to 0.212 in 2000. However, up to 2004 it decreased to 0.207 again. Compared to this, following figures arose for Germany: marginal quota of consumption: 0.57; marginal investment quota: from 1995 to 2000 each about 0.215, from 2001 to 2004 on-going decline to 0.1925. Hereby Germany's investment weakness since 2001 compared to other EU-countries is revealed.

6 For an analysis of sectoral effects: Dieckheuer (2004), (2005); Hild (2004).

exogenous because the exports and imports of the other countries of the world are not an integral part of the model.

Figure 3: Effects on sectoral employment and value added (1995 = 100)

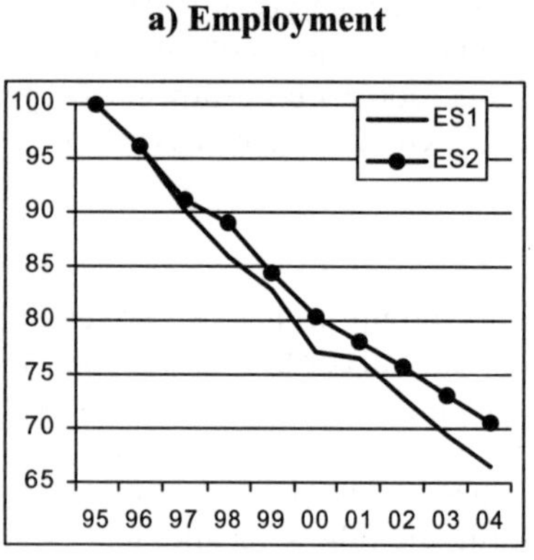

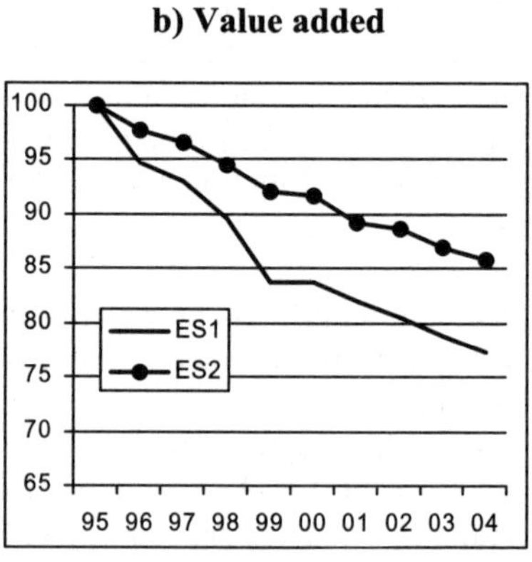

Figure 3 shows the development of the effect on employment and value added for the years 1995 to 2004. Both effects decline over time. An increase in exports in sector ES1 induces an employment effect in 2004 which falls about 35% short of those in the year 1995 and an effect on value added which is about 23% lower than in 1995. In case of an increase of exports in sector ES2 the employment effect in 2004 is about 30% and the effect on value added about 15% lower than in 1995. These developments are caused by changes in labour productivity as well as changes in the input coefficients of the intermediate inputs on the one hand and evoked by an outsourcing of parts of the value chain towards other sectors within Germany respectively by a national outsourcing on the other hand.

From figure 4 one can see that labour productivity and the import coefficient have increased in both sectors between 1995 and 2004. However, the increase of both in the main export sector ES1 was higher than in sector ES2. Therefore, the above considered distinctions in the development of the effect on employment and value added can be explained. The effects of national outsourcing are treated beneath.

Figure 4: Labor productivity and import-coefficient in the export-sectors (1995 = 100)

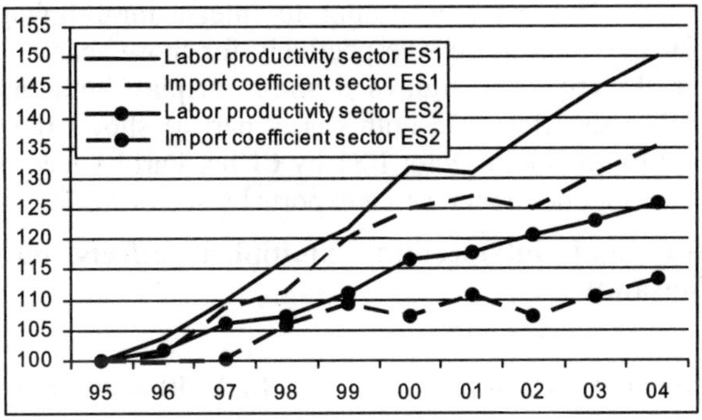

Figure 5 displays the multiplier effects with respect to employment and value added. An increase in exports in the main sector ES1 by €1 bn is followed by a rise in this sector's employment by 11910 employees in 1995 and by merely 7930 employees in 2004. In case of an increase in exports in sector ES2 by €1 bn these effects were fairly higher (14540 in 1995 and 10250 employees in 2004). With regard to the multiplier effects on value added, an increase in exports by the sector ES1 induces an increase of € 540 m in 1995 and € 410 m in 2004 within this sector. In sector ES2 a rise in exports causes a bigger impact on the value added with an increase of about € 580 m in 1995 and € 500 m in 2004.

Figure 5: Intrasectoral multiplier effects on employment and value added

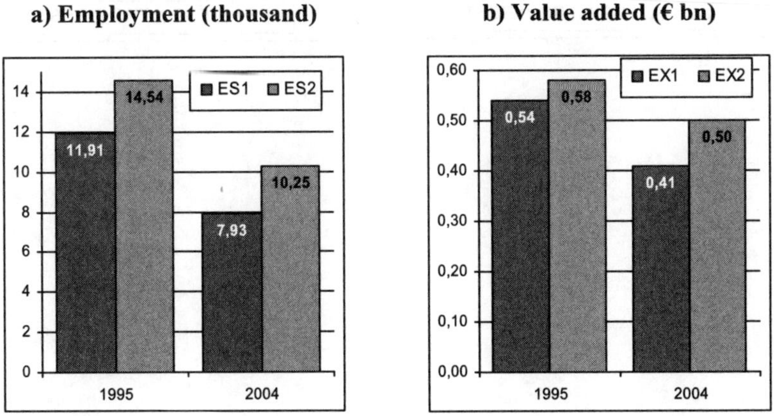

4.2 Intersectoral spill-over-effects

As figure 5 shows, intrasectoral effects on employment and value added are comparatively low. However, according to intersectoral linkages spill-over-effects occur for the other sectors respectively for those sectors whose exports do not increase directly. The figures 6 and 7 display both intrasectoral and intersectoral spill-over-effects. In both cases, part a) shows the effects on the exports' increase by the main sector ES1 by €1 bn. Part b) accordingly presents the impacts occurring due to increasing exports by sector ES2.

Figure 6: Intra- and intersectoral multiplier effects on employment (thousand)

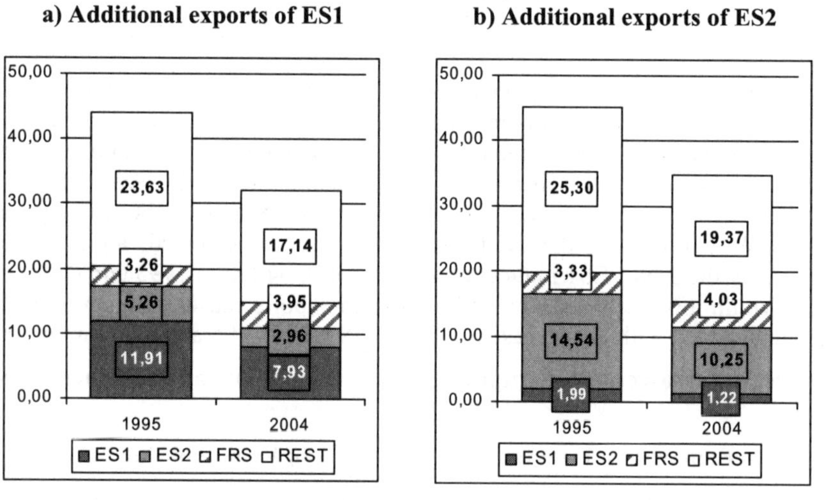

Figure 7: Intra- and intersectoral multiplier effects on value added (€ bn)

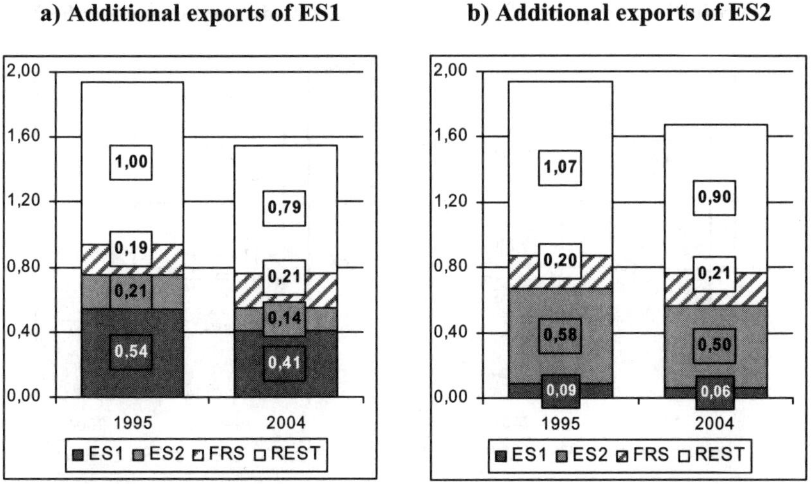

The following becomes apparent:

- Spill-over-effects have a greater impact on employment and value added than intersectoral effects have.
- The total effect on employment and value added between 1995 and 2004 has declined significantly.
- The effects in sector FRS (firm related services) developed in the opposite direction than the trend.

The increase in effects in sector FRS is caused by the outsourcing of sectors ES1 and ES2. This led mainly to a shift of parts of the value chain towards the sector of firm related services (FRS). In detail this includes services in the area of research, development (IT-development and support, production design etc.), consulting, hardware support and commercial cleaning.

Figure 8 presents both sectors' portions of total employment effects. It becomes apparent that shares of the export-focused sectors ES1 and ES2 both have declined significantly. In contrast, the sector of firm related services (FRS) reveals a remarkable increase of its share. It rose from 7.4% in 1995 to 12.3% respectively 11.6% in 2004. The other sectors' (REST) share has not changed much or has only declined faintly.

On the one hand the increase of the FRS sectors' share can be explained by the above described outsourcing-effect. On the other hand it results from the lower increase in labour productivity in sector FRS compared to the export-focused sectors.

Figure 8: Sectoral shares of employment effects (%)

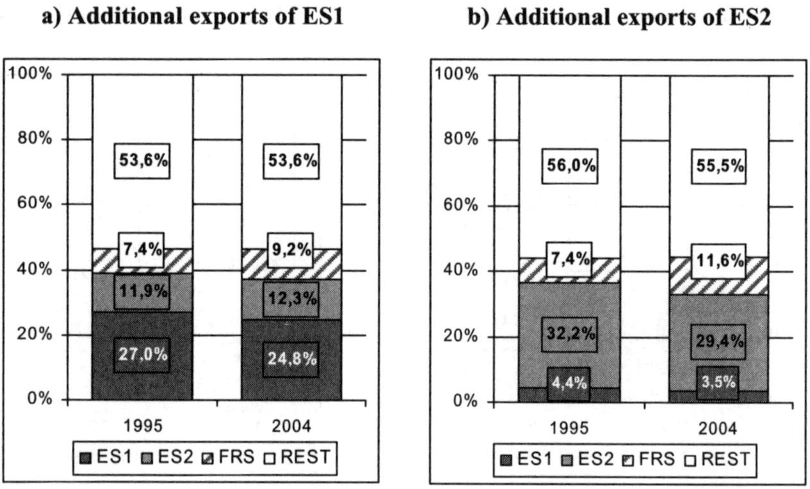

5 Macroeconomic effects in Germany and the EU-25

The sectoral analysis has demonstrated that the effects of additional exports on value added and employment in the German export-oriented sectors ES1 and ES2 have decreased considerably between 1995 and 2004. Although this decrease was alleviated through national spill-over-effects thesc could not compensate it completely. Accordingly, the macroeconomic effects on gross domestic product and employment have decreased in Germany in the considered period of time. Figure 9 illustrates this. As already demonstrated in the previous analysis the effects are again triggered by an exogenous rise of exports in the amount of €1 bn in each year either by the main export sector ES1 or by the other important export-oriented sector ES2.

In case of an export increase of ES1 the effect on GDP decreases by approximately 20% and the effect on employment by about 27.5% between 1995 and 2004. If exports of sector ES2 rise, the decline amounts to approximately 15% and 23%, respectively. The fact that there is a lower decline in the second case can be explained by the changes in labour productivity and import coefficients. Both variables have increased far more in sector ES1 than in sector ES2 (see figure 4).

Figure 9: Effects on GDP and total Employment in Germany (1995 = 100)

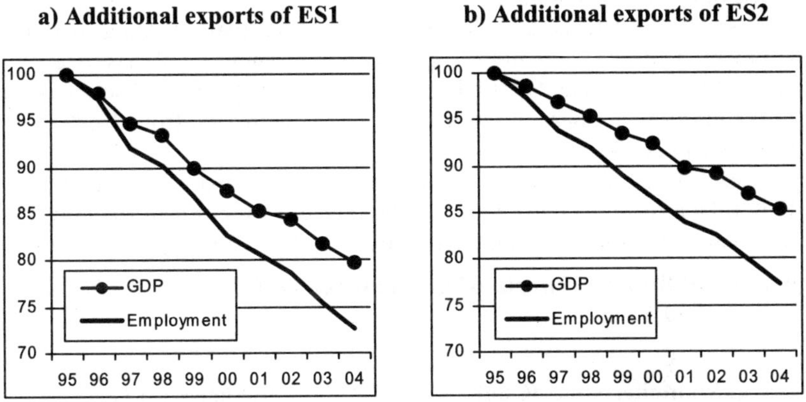

Although the effect of additional sectoral exports on GDP has decreased between 1995 and 2004, GDP has continued to increase considerably in 2004. Adherent to this was a rise in domestic absorption and accordingly in domestic demand for consumption and investment goods which amongst other things led to an increase in direct imports especially of consumer goods. Consequently it came to an increase both in sectoral imports of intermediate inputs and in direct imports between 1995 and 2004. Because of the rise of the sectoral import coefficients as well as the coefficients regarding direct imports in the considered period of time total German imports have increased far stronger than German GDP. Great effects on GDP and employment in the remaining EU-25 countries have emanated from these imports. To clarify this, the total effects, which are initiated by additional autonomous exports of the German export-oriented sector ES1 within the EU-25, will be examined below. These refer to exports into the rest of the world so that the actual stimulus of the exports does not have a direct effect on the countries of the EU-25, except for Germany. The second case of an autonomous increase in exports by the sector ES2 discussed above will not be illustrated here because in terms of the spill-over-effects in the EU-25 there are no new aspects.

Figure 10 shows that the total GDP-effect ceases but that there are remarkable spill-over-effects in the other countries of the EU-25, nevertheless. In detail the following findings can be identified:

- A €1 bn per year increase of the autonomous exports of sector ES1 raised the GDP of total EU-25 in 1995 by an amount of approximately €3 bn and in 2004 by an amount of more than €2.5 bn. Although the income multiplier has decreased it still remains quite high in 2004.

- The German share of the GDP-effect has decreased from 70.8% in 1995 to 66.5% in 2004. Compared to this, the shares in the three considered groups of the other EU-25-countries did increase.
- The spill-over-effects are the highest for the main trading partners of Germany (for the EU-country group EUA). Their GDP has risen by an amount of € 560 bn and € 500 bn, respectively. Despite the absolute decrease of the effect their share in the total effect has increased from 18.7% in 1995 to 19.6% in 2004.
- The spill-over into the new EU-countries is quite remarkable (country group EUC). Due to the achievements in the course of the transformation process the share in the total effect increased from 2.4% in 1995 to 4.2% in 2004.

Figure 10: Additional exports of German sector ES1 - GDP-effects within the EU-25

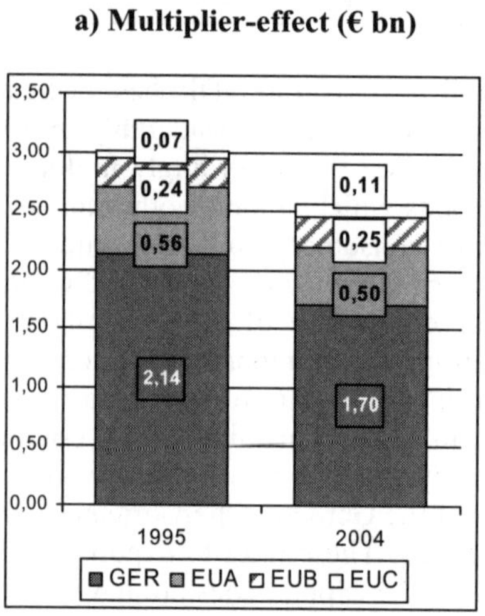

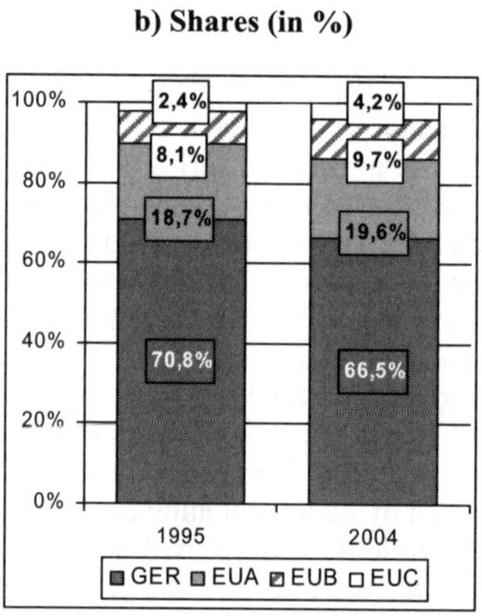

The GDP-effect in all the EU-25-countries which is caused by the autonomous rise of exports in Germany is at about the same level as in 1995, being about € 860 m in 2004. On the other hand there was a relatively high decline of the GDP-effect from € 2.14 bn to € 1.70 bn within Germany. In the first instance, this can be explained by the relatively high increase of the German import quotas as well as by the increasing importance of the new EU-countries' trade with the other EU-countries and particularly with Germany. Against this background Germany has "exported" a persistently higher share of its GDP-effect into the other EU-countries. However, this is a completely normal development within the European integration process. Due to the significant repercussion effects in the scope of the export-import-linkages within the EU-25 notable multiplicative amplifications of the effects arise which also benefit Germany.

Owing to the fact that there is a close connection between employment and GDP the findings concerning these two variables are vastly similar. Nonetheless few differences can be observed in figure 11:

- The employment effect in the EU-countries except Germany has decreased from about 24500 additional employed persons in 1995 to about 21800 additional employees in 2004. This was also caused by the relatively high increase of the labour productivity in the other EU-25 countries.
- However, the increase in productivity was much higher in Germany than in the other countries of the EU-25. Together with the previously mentioned spill-over-effects concerning the GDP a quite high "export" of employment into the other EU-countries resulted. The share of these countries in the total employment effect increased from 35.7% in 1995 to 40.5% in 2004.
- The employment share has increased especially in the new EU-countries. This was also caused by the achievements made in the transformation process. Compared to the above displayed GDP-shares the shares in employment of the new EU-countries are relatively high. This is mirrored by the prevailing relative low labour productivity in these countries.

Figure 11: Additional exports of German sector ES1 – Employment effects within the EU-25

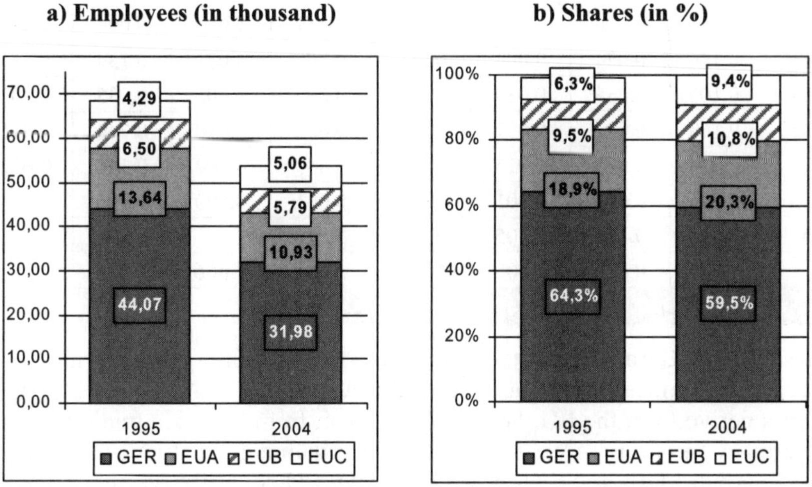

6 Sectoral and macroeconomic interdependencies in 2004

To convey an insight in the complex linkages which result from the above displayed effects within Germany and the whole EU-25, the effects of an autonomous increase of exports by the main German export-oriented sector ES1 for the year 2004 will be outlined below. Table 5 illustrates the intrasectoral, intersectoral and macroeconomic effects within Germany. In table 6 the international effects in the EU-25 are displayed.

The stimulus is triggered by the autonomous increase of demand of the countries belonging to the category of rest of the world for products of the German sector ES1 in the amount of €1 bn (tagged amount in table 5). Due to the international interdependencies the exports of this sector ultimately increase by an amount of € 1.031 bn (see table 5). The production value of the sector ES1 rises by an amount of € 1.437 bn. In the scope of the national interdependencies displayed in table 5, production in the other sectors also rises so that the increase of total production value amounted to € 3.589 bn. In the context of this production effect employment and GDP in Germany also rise. The number of employees moved upward in all sectors by 31978 and the GDP increased by €1.704 bn. Moreover, the additional production induced imports by an amount of € 632 m. By this, there is caused a transmission effect to the other countries of the EU-25.

Table 5: Sectoral and macroeconomic effects in Germany 2004

(€ bn; employment in thousand)

	ES1	ES2	FRS	REST	Σ	EX	DA	Σ
ES1	0.282	0.006	0.001	0.022	0.311	1.031	0.096	1.437
ES2	0.146	0.074	0.004	0.056	0.279	0.023	0.134	0.435
FRS	0.105	0.033	0.038	0.089	0.264	0.002	0.035	0.302
REST	0.169	0.092	0.037	0.363	0.661	0.010	0.744	1.415
IM	0.315	0.086	0.015	0.069	0.485	0.000	0.146	**0.632**
TS	0.005	0.001	0.001	0.023	0.031	0.000	0.116	
VA	0.415	0.144	0.205	0.794	1.558	–	–	
Σ	1.437	0.435	0.302	1.415	3.589	**1.066**	1.270	
E	7.930	2.956	3.949	17.143	31.978			

The additional German imports spread to the three country groups of the EU-25 (except for Germany) and the rest of the world (RW). About 64% of these imports derive from the EU, here from € 201 m from the main trading partners of Germany (group EUA), € 135 m from the remaining countries of the original EU-15 (group EUB) and € 68 m from the new EU-countries (group EUC). Out of this, production effects arise in all countries of the EU. Thereby exports and imports in trade between the EU-countries increased by an amount of € 634 m. In line with the export-import-coherences the GDP in all EU-countries increases (additional € 501 m in the group EUA, € 249 m in the EUB-group and € 108 m in the EUC-group). The GDP of the EU-25 rised by € 2592 bn in total. The income multiplier of an autonomous export increase thus amounts 2.592.

Table 6: Export-Import-linkages in the EU-25 in 2004 (€ bn; employment in thousand)

	GER	EUA	EUB	EUC	Σ	RW	EX	DA	FD
GER	–	0.030	0.021	0.015	0.066	**1.000**	**1.066**	1.270	2.336
EUA	0.201	0.037	0.038	0.011	0.287	0.000	0.287	0.395	0.682
EUB	0.135	0.035	0.019	0.008	0.197	0.000	0.197	0.167	0.364
EUC	0.068	0.005	0.005	0.007	0.084	0.000	0.084	0.097	0.181
RW	0.228	0.074	0.034	0.032	0.367				
IM	**0.632**	0.180	0.116	0.073	1.001				
GDP	1.704	0.501	0.249	0.108	**2.562**				
FD	2.336	0.682	0.364	0.181	3.563				
E	31.978	10.929	5.786	10.121	58.814				

From the production and the income effects repercussions arise on Germany. The imports of the country groups EUA, EUB and EUC from Germany have increased by € 66 m. This still induces a rise of the German GDP in the amount of € 114 m.

Production and income effects in the EU also lead to reactions in Germany. The imports of country groups EUA, EUB and EUC coming from Germany increased by €66 m in total. This still induced an increase of € 114 m of the German GDP.

The analysis reveals that in line with national and international interdependencies great effects evolve as a result of the autonomous increase in German exports. One third of the total GDP-effect and 45% of the whole employment effect disperse among the countries of the EU-25 excepting Germany. Besides, 7% of the effect on GDP and employment in Germany result from repercussions from the EU-25. The trade volume within the entire EU-25 rised by the amount of € 634 m. With regard to the underlying impulse of an autonomous export increase by €1 bn a great trade effect results consequently.

However, the production effect, the income effect and the employment effect are even higher in reality. These results from the fact that the entire EU-25 increases its imports from the rest of the world by € 367 m (see table 6). It is to be expected that additional positive repercussions will arise for all EU-countries. These effects are not included in the earlier analysis due to a lack of data. The

EU-25's high share in the world market leads to the assumption that the countries of the rest of the world would have raised their imports from the EU-25 by at least € 100 m as a result of the endogenous caused effects. This would eventually lead to an increase of the examined export impulse by at least further 10% and accordingly increase the production, income and employment effects in the EU-25 by a similar amount.

7 Summary

The shares of value added and employment in exports have continuously decreased in the period from 1995 to 2004 in all countries of the EU-25. Indeed, the attenuation was the greatest in the new EU-countries, mainly because of the special impacts of the transition process through which exceptionally high increases in productivity, especially in the export sectors, were achieved. Among the countries of the former EU-15 the strongest decrease of value added and employment shares of exports took place in Germany. This was primarily caused by the relatively high increases in labour productivities and import quotas in the German export-oriented sectors.

Against this background the effects of an autonomous increase in exports on sectoral and macroeconomic variables in the other EU-25 countries initiated by the most important export sectors in Germany are analysed in this paper. The theoretical and at the same time empirical analysis was undertaken on the base of an intersectoral model for Germany as well as an international model for the entire EU-25. Thereby the following outcomes resulted:

- Though an exogenous increase in the exports by the main export-oriented sectors in Germany led to a relatively minor positive intrasectoral employment and value added change, clearly positive spill-over-effects result from the national intersectoral linkages of these sectors. These impulses have a multiplicative strengthening effect on macroeconomic employment and value added as well as on GDP in Germany itself.
- The spill-over-effects within Germany were mainly associated to a notable shift of parts of the value added chain from the export-oriented sectors to the predominantly domestic-oriented sectors of firm related services. Contrary to the trend, positive developments of value added and employment effects yielded in the total period between 1995 and 2004.
- The relatively high import quotas of the main export-oriented sectors in Germany imply considerable effects in the EU-countries outside of Germany. Out of this, repercussions result having a positive impact on the German economy as a whole. Such effects and repercussions have been included in the analysis as endogenously for the entire EU-25. From the intrasectoral, intersectoral and international linkages follows that owing to autonomous export increases in 2004 an export multiplier of 2.5 in the entire

EU-25 arises, that is to say that an increase of the autonomous export sector by €1 bn leads to an increase of the GDP of the EU-25 in the amount of €2.5 bn. Due to the relatively high increase of productivity the employment effect turned out lower than the GDP-effect, but nonetheless a remarkable increase in employment in the EU-25 resulted as well.

- The effects from Germany on GDP and employment in the other countries of the EU have continuously strengthened between 1995 and 2004. In the year 2004 these countries obtained 33% of the total GDP effect and 40% of the total employment effect caused by additional exports coming from the German export-oriented sectors. This consequently led to spill-over-effects from Germany into the EU-25.
- Despite the above shown development, Germany is not expected to mutate into a "bazaar-economy" in a conceivable period of time. The export-oriented sectors have proceeded largely in substituting domestic by international production, but nevertheless they contribute to an important extent to employment and value added in the other German sectors and therefore in whole German economy. One will have to accustom oneself to the fact that employment and value added effects will decrease within the scope of the globalisation process in the traditional sectors of the German manufacturing industry because parts of the value added chain will be displaced abroad and thereupon domestic products will be replaced by imported foreign products. This exactly, though, is an indispensable condition for the emergence and expansion of new markets in the expanded EU as well as worldwide, which on their part open up export prospects for Germany.

Literature

Brautzsch, H.-U. and Ludwig, U. (2004): Verliert der deutsche Export an gesamtwirtschaftlicher Antriebskraft?, in: Wirtschaft im Wandel, 10. Vol., pp. 435-442.

Brautzsch, H.-U. and Ludwig, U. (2005): Ganz Westeuropa auf dem Weg in die Basarökonomie?, in: Wirtschaftsdienst, 85. Vol., pp. 513-517.

Clement, R. and Natrop, J. (2004): Offshoring- Chance oder Bedrohung für den Standort Deutschland?, in: Wirtschaftsdienst, 84. Vol., pp. 519-528.

Dieckheuer, G., (2004): Außenhandel, Wertschöpfung und Beschäftigung. Untersuchungen mit einem Input-Output-Modell für Deutschland, in: Volkswirtschaftliche Diskussionsbeiträge der Universität Münster No. 357, Münster.

Dieckheuer, G., (2004): Der Beitrag der Textil- und Bekleidungsindustrie zu Wertschöpfung, Beschäftigung und Außenhandel in Deutschland. Fakten und Perspektiven zu den intrasektoralen, intersektoralen und gesamtwirtschaftlichen Verflechtungen und Wirkungen, in: FATM-Studie, Münster.

Eurostat (2005): Macroeconomic data for the EU (from Datastream).

Flassbeck, H. (2004): Basar-Ökonomie oder Basar-Ökonomen?, in: Wirtschaft und Markt, Berlin.

Hild, R. (2004): Produktion, Wertschöpfung und Beschäftigung im Verarbeitenden Gewerbe, in: ifo Schnelldienst, 57. Vol., No. 7, pp. 19-27.

Holub, H.-W. and Schnabl, H. (1994): Input-Output-Rechnung, München.

Horn, G. and Behncke, S. (2004): Deutschland ist keine Basarökonomie, in: DIW Wochenbreicht, 71. Vol., pp. 583-589.

International Monetary Fund (2005): Direction of Trade Statistics, Washington, D.C.

IWD (2003): Deutschland und der Weltmarkt – vom Standort entkoppelt, in: iwd Informationsdienst der deutschen Wirtschaft, No. 51/52, Köln.

Leontief, W. (1987): Input-Output-Analysis, in: The New Palgrave. A Dictionary of Economics, Vol. 2, New York, pp. 860-864.

Miller, E. and Blair, P.D. (1985): Input-Output-Analysis: Foundations and Extensions, Englewood Cliffs.

Schintke, J. and Weiß, J.P. (2003): Zunehmende Außenhandelsverflechtung: Kompensieren sich Beschäftigungseffekte von Export- und Importsteigerungen?, in: DIW Wochenbericht No. 9.

Schneider, St. (2004): Deutschlands Basarökonomie: Mehr Leistung – oder der Zug geht weiter ins Ausland!, Deutsche Bank Research.

Schumann, J. (1968),:Input-Output-Analyse. Berlin-Heidelberg.

Sinn, H.W. (2005): Basar-Ökonomie Deutschland. Exportweltmeister oder Schlusslicht?, in: Ifo-Schnelldienst, No. 6.

Statistisches Bundesamt (2002): Volkswirtschaftliche Gesamtrechnungen, Input-Output-Tabellen in Preisen von 1995, 1991 bis 2000, Wiesbaden.

Statistisches Bundesamt (2004): Volkswirtschaftliche Gesamtrechnungen, Input-Output-Rechnung 2000, Wiesbaden.

Statistisches Bundesamt (2005a): Statistisches Jahrbuch für die Bundesrepublik Deutschland, Wiesbaden.

Statistisches Bundesamt (2005b): Statistisches Jahrbuch für das Ausland, Wiesbaden.

Benchmarking International Employment and Growth Performance: The Bertelsmann Foundation Approach

by
Ulrich van Suntum

1 Introduction

Every two years, the Bertelsmann foundation publishes its International Business Location Ranking ("Internationales Standortranking").[1] This is a benchmarking project which compares growth and employment in the 21 leading industrial nations. An overall analysis of strengths and weaknesses is conducted, examining the underlying causes and identifying successful solutions. Proposals derived from the International Business Location Ranking provide a variety of potential strategies for the respective countries and, in particular, for Germany. The proposals concentrate on the labour market, the government and general economic conditions, as well as business-workforce relations. The "Success Index" provides information on the current situation in each country with regard to two target areas: the labour market (unemployment rates and increases in the number of employees entering the workforce) and growth (per capita gross domestic product and potential growth). In addition, an "Activity Index" is provided, which evaluates and quantifies the specific measures which the individual countries have used to stimulate their labour markets and economic growth. The analysis thus indicates potential areas for policy and intervention.

Since 2005, the Ranking has been supplemented by a six-monthly "business check", which is applied to a selected economic topic. The first business check in spring 2005 dealt with youth unemployment, while the second in autumn 2005 focuses on the problem of public debt. Moreover, the business check provides a brief overview of the most recent economic developments and the implications of current ranking figures. Another project on behalf of the Bertelsmann Foundation, which will be discussed later in this paper, deals with the economic performance of eight Eastern European Economies including Poland.

2 Methodology and main results of the Bertelsmann Business Location Ranking

The general outcome of the latest ranking yielded a depressing result for Germany, which ranked last of 21 countries. Interestingly, the four major conti-

[1] Hafemann / van Suntum (2004a).

nental European countries – Spain, Italy, France and Germany – were together at the bottom of the list. By contrast, the three Anglo-Saxon countries of Ireland, the USA and Australia, achieved the top rankings, with other liberal economies such as Great Britain and New Zealand also doing quite well. The Scandinavian countries had somewhat mixed results. While Norway and Denmark fared reasonably well, Finland was in the "red zone"[2] of the ranking list.

Figure 1: Bertelsmann Ranking List 2004

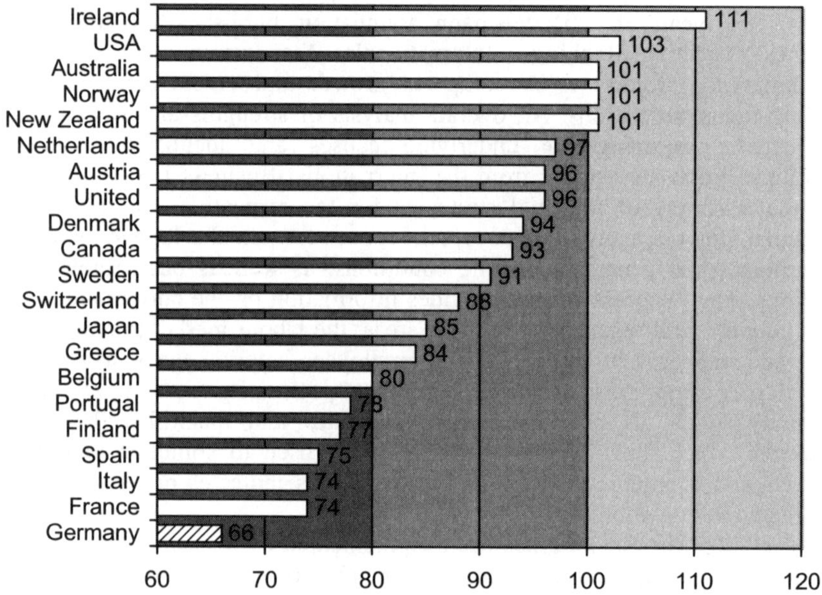

Germany's performance has deteriorated continuously since the early nineties. This is not simply a result of the unification, as one might assume. Indeed, unification *has* caused a lower average per capita GDP in Germany, because of the lower income prevailing in the former GDR. Yet, one would in fact have expected *higher* growth rates after the unification. Unfortunately, however, this optimistic vision did not materialize. Therefore, there must have been some severe mistakes in economic policy for which the unification is not responsible.

At this point, some words on the methodological background of the ranking seem appropriate. The list itself indicates the so-called index of success, which contains four statistics:

- per capita GDP as a rough measure of welfare;

---

[2] Here dark grey.

- economic growth, which is measured by potential, rather than current rises in GDP;
- the unemployment rate, as standardized by the OECD
- employment growth as a dynamic measure of the labour market.

All these variables are published regularly by the OECD. Our investigation covers the 17 years between 1986 and 2003. Hence, with 21 countries, there are 357 figures for each variable which can be used for the econometrics underlying the investigation.

The ranking not only reflects the pure economic results, but also attempts to explain why some countries perform better than others. This is done by means of the activity index, consisting of an additional set of 16 variables. These are divided into three subsets, labelled "labour market", "business cycle and public economy" and "business sector and collective bargaining".

Figure 2: Activity Index

Activity Index

Labour market	**Business cycle and public economy**	**Business sector and collective bargaining**
• Long term unemployment (-) • Youth unemployment (-) • Unemployment of older people (-) • Participation rate	• Government outlays/GDP (-) • Public debt/GDP (-) • Marginal rates of income tax and contributions (-) • Economic situation	• Gross fixed capital formation /GDP • Part-time labour • Moderate wage policy • Strikes

Some of the sub-variables should be explained in more detail. For example, youth unemployment and unemployment of older workers refer to the respective **deviations** from the overall level of unemployment. Interestingly, Germany is one of only three countries in which older workers have a higher unemployment rate than the average for the entire population (the other two countries being Japan and Austria). On the other hand, youth unemployment is not too a severe problem in Germany, unlike in many other countries.

Moderate wage policy is measured by the nominal growth of GDP minus nominal wage increases. The simple concept behind this measure is that increases in personal wages should not, on average and in the long run, exceed the increase in total output. There is some econometric evidence that this measure can, at least to a certain extent, explain international differences in rates of unemployment and of employment growth.

Empirical evidence was provided by means of an econometric pool analysis. It exhibited very close correlations between the 16 sub-variables of the activity index and one or more of the four success index variables.

Figure 3: Correlation of success index and activity index over time (Germany)

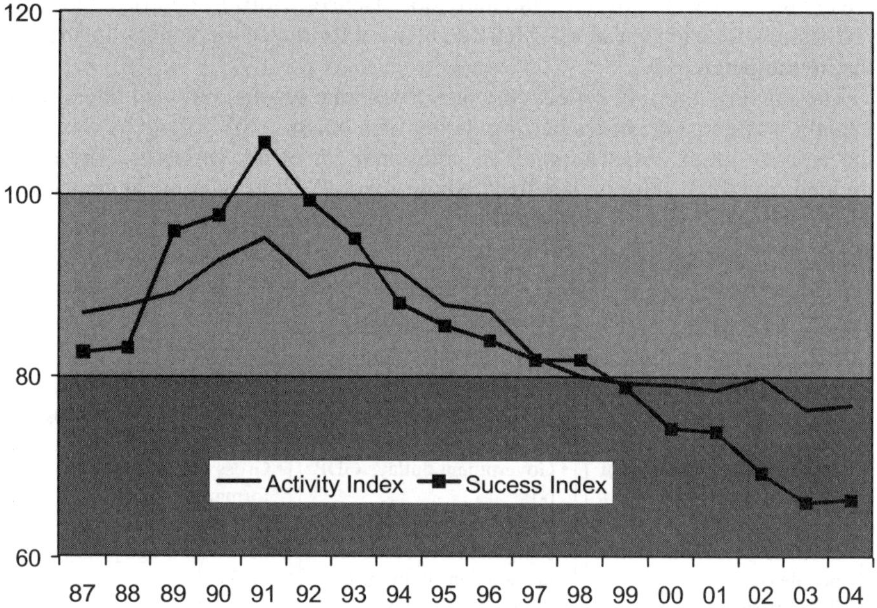

There is also a high level of correlation between the success and activity indexes as a whole. This applies to both cross sectional data for the 21 counties and also along the time axis for each individual country.Each variable is converted to points between 0 and 120, where high points represent good performance and vice versa. In order to obtain these points, variables are transformed by a logistic function, so that extreme values are partially absorbed and do not distort the measurement. The benchmark for each individual criterion is the average of the three best-performing countries. In the next step, three rating-zones are defined:

Figure 4: Rating-Zones

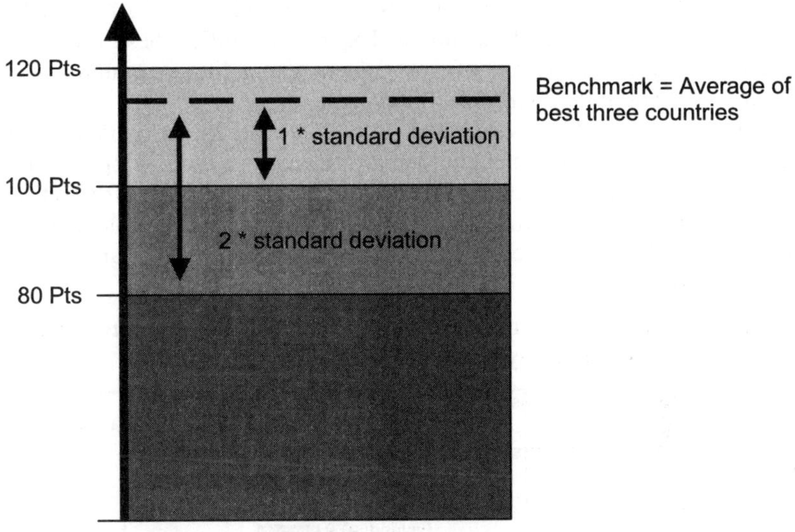

- benchmark minus standard-deviation of the entire set = end of the green zone (light grey)
- benchmark minus twice the standard-deviation = beginning of the red zone (dark grey)
- points score between the green (light grey) and the red zone (dark grey) = yellow zone (grey)

This evaluation scheme is applied to each variable as well as to the overall ranking position of the respective countries and therefore provides an unequivocal and unique rating procedure, which has already been replicated in the benchmarking literature.

3 Germany's economic performance in the light of the ranking

There have been substantial changes in the relative positions of the countries over time.Ireland, for example, was in the red (dark grey) zone for years and now leads the ranking list. Great Britain and New Zealand have developed in a similarly positive manner. In contrast, the positions of some continental European countries including Germany and Portugal have deteriorated over the last ten years, and they are now at the bottom of the list. Switzerland scores well on employment, but suffers from poor growth rates.

One of Germany's main economic weaknesses is its low rate of investment, the result of high wage rates, excessive regulation, high taxes and social welfare contributions. There is also an unduly high level of public debt in Germany. The official debt/GDP ratio of 67% does not even include implicit debt hidden in the social systems, which amounts to no less than approximately 270% of GDP, as estimated by the Council of Economic Experts in 2003. These problems are accompanied by a high share of government expenditures (roughly 47% of GDP) and substantial long-term unemployment.

One of the most striking weaknesses in the German labour market is the low participation rate and high unemployment rate amongst older people. The main reasons are automatic wage increases with increasing age, early retirement schemes (which are now being gradually reduced) and special protection against dismissal for older employees, which has prevailed for many years and is now slowly being removed.

Figure 5: Unemployment of older people in 2003 (divergence from the general unemployment rate in percentages)

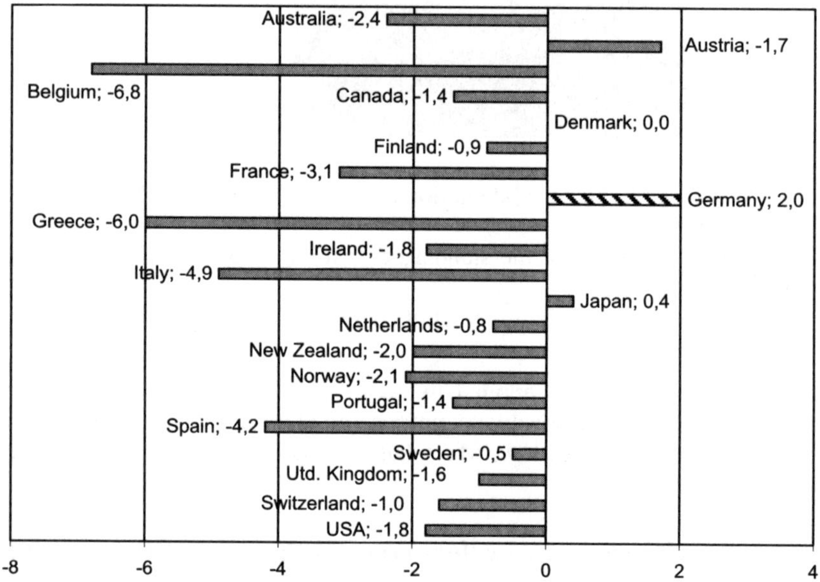

Of course, not everything is bad in Germany. One can point to the excellent educational system for apprentices, which explains the relatively low youth unemployment rate, in comparison with other countries. Traditionally, there is also a high level of social consensus, resulting, for example, in relatively low strike rates. Moreover, the high share of small and medium-size enterprises remain an important asset to the German economy. These firms supply no less than 70% of the total number of jobs and are consistently much more innovative and flexible than their larger counterparts.

4 Performance of Central and Eastern European Countries

As mentioned above, in 2004, the Bertelsmann foundation published a study on the Eastern European countries, focussing particularly on those which have recently entered the EU. Like the Bertelsmann business location ranking, this study was also developed by the Centre of applied Economics in Münster (CAWM).[3]

The two studies had similar methodologies, although growth and income have not yet been taken into account in assessing the Eastern European countries. The relatively short time period for which data was available also led to less sophisticated and reliable results in case of the Eastern European study.

Figure 6: Unemployment Rates in Eastern-European Countries

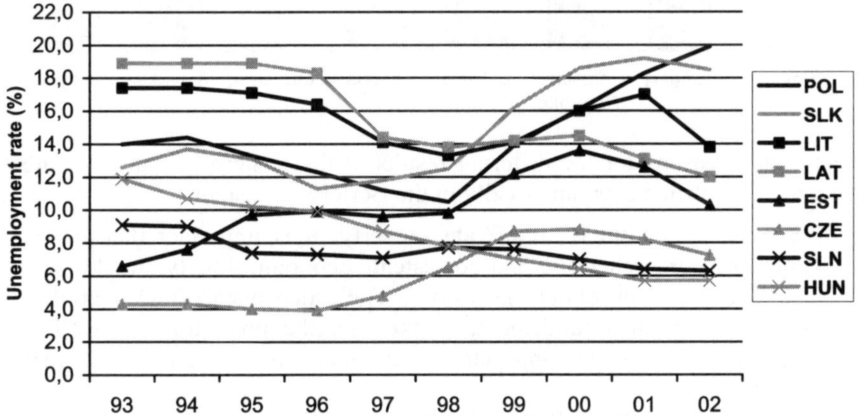

The transformation process of the former centrally planned economies since 1990 has revealed their considerable lack of efficiency and competitiveness in comparison with the Western industrial countries. This initially caused massive job-losses and declining incomes. In the mid 90's the situation began to improve substantially, but then worsened again.

As in the case of the Western industrial states, however, the economic performance of the Eastern European countries has also varied considerably. Between 1993 and 2003, Slovenia and Hungary did very well. Poland, unfortunately, has the poorest performance with respect to unemployment rates. It is located at the bottom of our Eastern European ranking list and could, therefore, be described as "the Germany of the East".

3 Hafemann / van Suntum (2004b).

Figure 7: Eastern European Ranking List (2003)

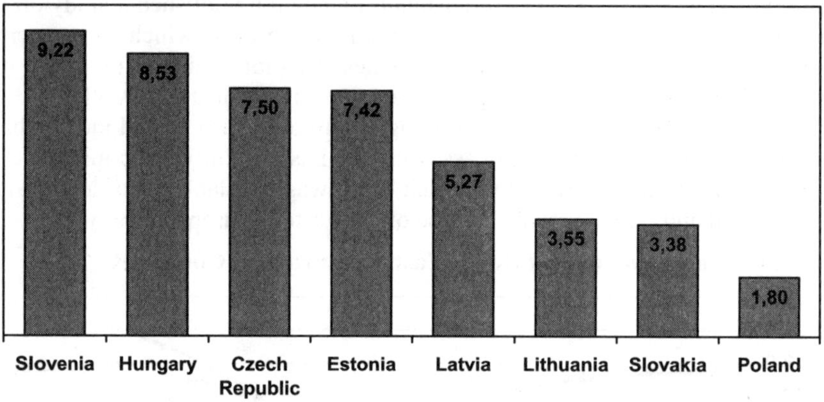

Three main reasons for the differing results of the Eastern European countries have been identified econometrically in the Bertelsmann study.

- Legal system & safety of private property. It is important that any legal system be comprehensive and consistent. Economic liberty should only be restricted where absolutely necessary. The independence and neutrality of the courts are also fundamental. Likewise, the protection of intellectual property rights is an important requirement for a functioning market economy.
- Corruption: the elimination and prevention of corruption fosters reliability and reduces the risks associated with investment. The relevant data came from the corruption perception index compiled by Transparency International. In this list, Germany ranks 16th with 7.7 points, while Poland ranks 64th with 3.6 points.
- Access to stable money: the lack of stable money erodes monetary wealth and raises the risks of long-term contracting. It therefore tends to reduce saving and investment.These three criteria were integrated into the overall ranking list, weighted with 50%, the other 50% stemming from labour-market-performance (unemployment rates and employment growth).

Figure 8: Ranking Positions of Eastern European Countries 1995 -2003

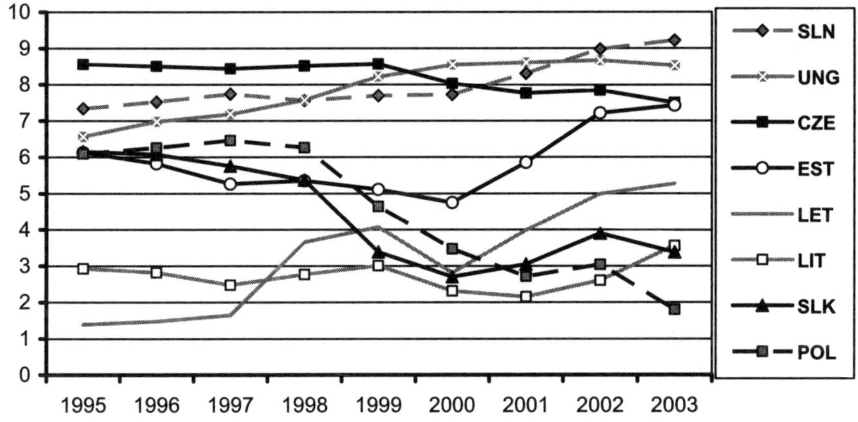

While Poland's position has deteriorated constantly since 1997, Estonia and Latvia have made considerable progress in the last three years. Slovenia, Hungary and the Czech Republic have held the three pole positions since the very beginning, from 1995 to 2003.

Nonetheless, Poland need not be unduly concerned about its low rank. There are many factors which were not integrated into the benchmarking process. Also, after entering the EU, the entire situation has changed in many respects. Last but not least, as in the case of Germany, having the lowest rank means that things can only get better!

Literature

Hafemann, K. and van Suntum, U., supported by Dorenkamp, C., Rottmann, J., Rückert, M. and Schlotböller, D. (2004a): Internationales Standort-Ranking 2004, Gütersloh.

Hafemann, K. and van Suntum, U., supported by Schlotböller, D. (2004b): Beschäftigungspolitik in Osteuropa, Gütersloh.

Foreign Direct Investment and the Labour Market in Poland

by

Jan Rymarczyk and Jerzy Rymarczyk

1 Theoretical basis for foreign direct investment (FDI)

Foreign direct investment may be interpreted theoretically by application of various micro and macro economic concepts [1].One may enumerate neo-factor theory and neo-technology theory, K. Kojima's theory which relates to the comparative costs theory, F.T. Knickerbocker's theory of following the competitors investing in foreign markets directly, R. Vernon's life cycle theory, and others. Undoubtedly, however, J.H. Duning's eclectic theory of international production explains this phenomenon best.

In order to address the FDI issue broadly he merged three theories which described their particular aspects, i.e. monopolistic benefits theory, localization theory and internalization theory. The first one claims that foreign investors tend to gain competitive advantage over local competition. This can be achieved thanks to advanced technologies, the know-how of modern organization and management methods, competitive advantage in marketing, supply chains, economies of scale, a strong brand, etc. These advantages are internalized by investors, i.e. they are used in branches and in sister companies (not so frequently in joint ventures) abroad. This enables them to avoid transaction costs related to export or sales and to monopolize knowledge and know how.

The third element of J.H. Duning's theory – localization theory - addresses the question why investors set up branches in country **X** and not in country **Y**, or why they do this more willingly and on a bigger scale than in the first one. The answer points to the fact that the country chosen by the investor possesses localization advantage, mainly better investment climate, cheaper production factors, well qualified workforce, resources, etc.

By combining those theories, J.H. Dunning drew the conclusion that the more competitive advantage a foreign investor has over a local competitor, the more stimuli there are to internalize these advantages. Likewise, the more profitable it is to take advantage of them abroad, the more involved the investor is.

Apart form J.H. Duning's theory it seems that Vernon's life cycle theory attempts to explain motives behind investors' activities for investing in Poland. After a product has been standardized, its production - due to comparative advantage (mainly the low costs of the work force) is moved to Poland. A broad and still unsaturated local market is another significant factor which leads to moving the production of goods to a branch in chosen country.

---

[1] See Rymarczyk (2004), pp. 33-56.

2 FDI in Poland

Influx of foreign capital to Poland has had a significant influence on the processes of transformation. Since its very beginning it has been very dynamic. The aggregate value of the FDI in Poland as at the end of 2003 was, according to the data published by the Polish Information and Foreign Investment Agency, 72.7b US-$ (according to National Polish Bank (NBP) it was US-$49 billion)[2]. This was one third of all foreign investment in the central and Eastern Europe. According to data published by UNCTAD Poland ranked first among those countries and ranked high in the first ten in the world. With an amount of 1253 US-$ per capita we are behind Czech Republic (3790 US-$), Estonia (3110 US-$), Hungary (3045 US-$), Slovenia (2011 US-$) and Slovakia (1586 US-$) (data as of 2002).

The year 2000 witnessed the biggest inflow of FDI, when over 10 billion US-$ was invested. The following years, however, witnessed a dramatic decrease which was mainly due to slowing down of the privatization process in Poland and much worse economic performance in the world.

Table 1: Direct Foreign Investment in Poland in the years 1993-2003

	Years										
Categories	**1993**	**1994**	**1995**	**1996**	**1997**	**1998**	**1999**	**2000**	**2001**	**2002**	**2003**
Amount of investment (in US-$ M)	2830	1491	2510	5197	5678	9574	7891	10601	7417	6064	6420
Dynamics[a]	-	52.6	168.3	207.0	109.3	168.6	82.4	134.3	67.4	84.8	105.9

[a] next year/previous year x 100

Source: Foreign Direct Investment in Poland in 2003 r., materials for the press conference of PAIiIZ, Warsaw, 15 of April 2004.

Most of the FDI was related to taking over state companies, and greenfield investment accounted for only a few percent. In the years 1990-2001 out of 315 privatized companies 101 investors were based abroad and 22 companies were joint venture companies.

In the years 1990-2002 most of the foreign capital was invested in the production sector – approx. 37%, financial sector – more than 26%, transportation and communication approx. 12% and trade – approx. 14% (data according to NBP).

2 Data published by different institutions (UNCTAD, GUS, NBP, PAIZ) vary significantly at times due to different calculation methods applied: if no other source has been given, FDI data comes from the annual reports of the Instytut Koniunktur i Cen Handlu Zagranicznego w Warszawie (Economic Trends and Foreign Trade Prices Institute).

Figure 1: Aggregate value of FDI in Poland in the years 1993-2003 (in US-$ M)

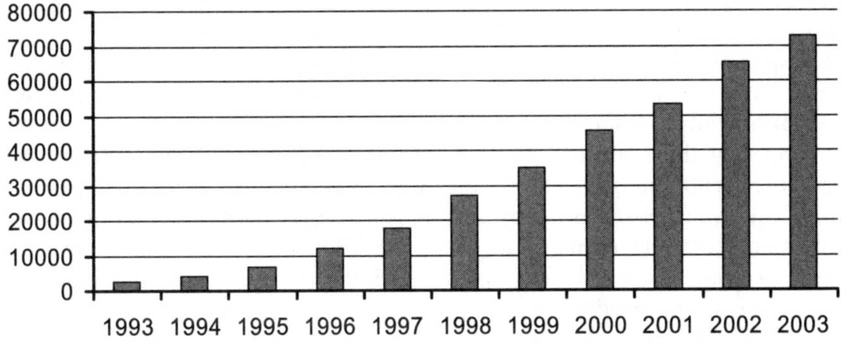

Source:FDI in Poland in 2003, materials for the press conference of PAIiIZ, Warsaw, 15 of April 2004.

In the banking sector the share of the foreign capital accounted for 60% (according to the data as at 2002); in the insurance sector approx. 72%. Out of 62 commercial banks in Poland 47 were controlled by foreign capital. The major investors in this sector included AVB, Citigroup, UniCredito Italiano, KBC Bank, Allied Irish Bank, Credit Agricole and ING Group NV. The fact that the banking sector has been dominated by foreign capital is subject to criticism and is considered to be one of the mistakes of privatization, as the most significant financial decisions are made outside Poland and they may be in conflict with the country's interest. Similarly, it is generally thought that domination of retail trade by major international hyper- and supermarket chains has brought many small Polish retailers to bankruptcy. The chains' importance is not due to their number but rather their scale and the new management strategies they apply. International trade corporations present on the Polish market, such as Metro AG, Casino Carrefour, Tesco and Jeronimi Martins Holding are on the list of 50 major foreign investors in Poland.

While criticizing the scale of privatization of Polish banks by foreign investors and greenfield investments in trade one must say, however, that without foreign investors Poland's economic efficiency would have been much lower.

The number of the foreign companies in the Polish economy does not reflect their importance. In 2002 there were more than 46 thousand foreign companies which accounted for 10% of all registered companies. The biggest share in terms of income was in the hotel and restaurant business (more than 48%), also in transportation, warehousing and communication sectors (45%), industry (39%), property management (30%) and financial services (28%).

In sectors such as production of tires (Goodyear, Michelin, Continental and Pirelli), telecommunication equipment (Siemens, Alcatel, Lucent Technologies,

Nokia, Ericsson), cars (Fiat, Daewoo, Volkswagen, General Motors, Renault etc.) food products for children (Ovita, Nutricia and Nestle), and delivery services (DHL, TNT, UPS, EMS) the level of oligopoly reached 80%.

Companies with foreign capital gave employment (as at the end of 2002) to over 1 million people, which meant that every fifth person worked for a foreign investor or a joint venture company.

Comparing the scale of employment with income generated indicates that companies with foreign capital were more efficient than their Polish competitors. They were also more profitable (despite applying transaction prices) and were more active in terms of investing. In 2002 their gross profitability was almost two times higher than companies with Polish capital only, and their share in investments exceeded 68%.

In terms of aggregate capital invested in Poland, Holland ranked first, followed by France, Germany, USA and Great Britain.

As stated above, global corporations play an important role. Out of the 1500 biggest firms form among the world's leading corporations by "Financial Times" 117 have invested in Poland, including 9 out of the biggest 10 (General Electric, Microsoft, Exxon Mobil, Citigroup, Pfizer, Intel, Johnson&Johnson, BP and Royal Dutch respectively). They account for 40% of aggregate FDI in Poland.

The biggest world's corporations, except Citigroup, do not however constitute the biggest investors in Poland. The biggest investors in Poland so far are the following: France Telecom (3.2b US-$), FIAT (1.7b US-$), Daewoo (1.6b US-$), HVB (1.4b US-$), Citigroup(1.3b US-$), Gazprom (1.3b US-$), Vivendi (1.2b US-$), United Pan-Europe Communications (1.2b US-$), UniCredito Italiano (1.1b US-$), Metro AG (1b US-$).

When discussing the influence of foreign investors on internationalizing of the Polish companies one must note that the influence is both direct and indirect. In the case of former Polish companies becoming branches of international corporations and becoming part of their strategy, this involves their restructuring in the scope of modern management, marketing, technology and employment. It should be noted, however, that international corporations do not usually transfer the latest technologies, but the middle-range technology which is more than average in Poland. In this way they extend the product's life cycle and avoid internal competition within the corporation. This refers particularly to joint ventures where the risk of innovation leakage is great. There is an exception to this rule, however, such as the production of elements and subcomponents which are used to assemble final products in other countries. They must conform to certain standards of the latest technology used in the corporation. This is the case within the automobile industry (e.g. assemblage of gear shifts for Toyota cars in Wałbrzych).

The above mentioned factors together with the lack of highly specialized labour, not enough investment in research and development centres translate into unwillingness of foreign investors to start B+R[3] activity in Poland. The fault can be partly attributed to Treasury Ministers who have neglected entering specific legal clauses into the agreements for privatization of attractive state companies. There are more and more cases, however, of foreign companies creating research and development centres, especially those related to IT (Oracle, Intel, Lucent Technologies, ABB and others) probably due to cost-related reasons.

Indirect impact is related to the *spill-over* effect and competition. Various domestic companies set up contacts with foreign companies. They act as suppliers, buyers and partners to those companies. Thanks to those contacts the latest technologies are transplanted together with the work practices. If a Polish company acts as a provider, a foreign company imposes certain values and standards so that the Polish partner can produce elements of the highest quality. Many companies have been forced by the competition to modernize and apply the newest technologies; to prove the above one may analyze the growing number of ISO 9000 certificates applied for by Polish companies.

FDI has undoubtedly led to the bankruptcy of many Polish state companies which could not cope with the competition; they were characterized by aging technologies, low product quality, high costs and poor marketing on the one hand, and strong labour unions on the other.

While entering the Polish market international companies used many different strategies. In the case of small and medium companies they applied rather traditional methods, involving setting up trade contacts (or less frequently co-operation) and setting up an agent or a network of agents, representatives, a joint venture or a sister company.

Big international companies started their activity on the Polish market signing trade contracts with the International Trade Centres before the transformation of the Polish economy. These were in the form of buyback transactions during the Gierek era, sales of licenses. After the fall of the Soviet block they set up branches in the form of sister companies on the basis of privatized companies. Some of them established a launch pad by setting up sister companies in Poland (Coca-Cola, PepsiCo, Danone, International Paper) or a chain of franchises (McDonald's, KFC)

The strategy adopted by international corporations in the first stage of their expansion (the first half of the 1990's) was multinational or global in nature[4].

---

[3] American Delphi and General Electric are the two exceptions; they have created Engineering Design Center co-operating with The Institute of Aviation in Warsaw.

[4] See Zorska (2002), pp.96-103.

Those companies provided goods tailored for the demands of the Polish market or, more frequently, standard products. In later stages one may notice also an international strategy which is based on co-operation (managed from the headquarters) with numerous branches located in central and Eastern Europe involving international work sharing.

The transition by international corporations to the practice of transnational strategy has resulted in applying its elements to their sister companies in Poland also.

3 The Labour market in Poland

The labour market in Poland in the 1990's and now is under the influence of demographic factors related to system transformation and changes in economic trends. In this respect the number of people of employable age grew (employed and unemployed) and their share of the population grew as well. In the 1990's people of employable age accounted for 57% of the population; in the 2001, however, for 62%. The end of the 1970's and the beginning of the 80's baby boom came of age, and at the same time people born in the boom after the World War II started to approach the retirement age [5].

Nevertheless, the greatest impact on the labour market and its most significant segment – unemployment – was exerted by system transformation. The transition from a centrally managed economy to a free market economy created a situation where hidden unemployment or overstaffing (economically unsound) in the state-run companies turned into conspicuous unemployment. Not only were the autonomous free market economy forces pushing unprofitable companies to bankruptcy or to rationalization, but there was also the purposeful activity of the government aiming at restructuring of the public sector. This was the case in the closing down of a number of former collective farms, which generated huge unemployment in many regions of the country, and with the restructuring of the steel industry and the state-owned railways.

The first wave of the unemployment came within a year from the start of the system changes. In December 1990 the number of the unemployed reached 1.1 million people and the rate of unemployment (registered) reached 6.5%. In the following years unemployment grew systematically, reaching a level of almost 3 million people in 1994, which translated into over 17% of the population of employable age. Better economic performance in 1995 resulted in a decrease of the number in the unemployed to 2.6 million people, and the rate of unemployment reached 13.1%[6].

---

[5] See Warsaw School of Economics (2003), pp.89-105.

[6] See Sucholiński (2002), pp. 38-42.

Figure 2: The unemployment rate in Poland in the years 1990-2002 in size and percent

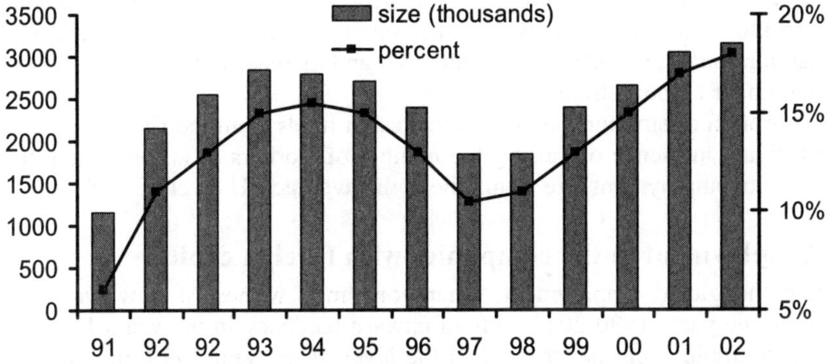

Source: The data published by the Main Statistical Office in Poland (various publications)

The positive changes in the labour market lasted until Autumn 1998 when unemployment remained at a level of 1.8 million people or 10.6%. In the following years unemployment rose steadily reaching the level of 3317000 people (18.1%) at the end of 2003. In November 2004 2943000 people remained jobless and the unemployment rate was at the level of 18.7%.

The second wave of the unemployment which started in September 1998 and which has lasted until now is related mainly to the worsening of economic performance and speeding up of the restructuring processes. There was a substantial workforce reduction in the private sector which, in the first years of the 21st century, accounted for almost 75% of its global size. Group redundancies which were on the rise in those years were the result of the fact that 3-5 year long work group agreements expired and the workers were no longer guaranteed safe workplace as was the case under formerly signed privatization agreements.

Table 2: The number of employed, the unemployed and the rate of unemployment in the years 1990- 2003 (as at the end of the year)

Details	**1990**	**1995**	**1998**	**1999**	**2000**	**2001**	**2002**	**2003**
Number of the unemployed (m)	1.12	2.63	1.83	2.35	2.7	3.12	3.3	3.3
Unemployment rate (%)	6.5	14.9	10.4	13.1	15	17.4	18.1	18.1
Number of the employed (m)	16.5	15.5	16.2	16	15.5	15	14.5	14.5

Source: Main Statistical Office, Poland (various publications).

The significant improvement in economic performance which took place in 2004 and the positive forecast for the coming years along with the opening of the labour markets in EU countries together with low demographic pressure may prompt one to conclude that even though unemployment in Poland has reached the highest level in the EU and OECD, it will steadily subside. One should also not underestimate a visible progress in education and the rising qualifications of the workforce in Poland, as well as the series of reforms aimed at liberalizing the labour market, reduction of labour costs and increased efficiency imposed on Poland under Lisbon Strategy.

Absorption of structural funds and cohesion funds from the EU will also have a significant influence on raising the number of workers. It is forecasted that in 2008 the unemployment rate should be at the average EU level of 10%

4 Employment in the companies with foreign capital

Unlike the global employment, where one may witness a downward trend, between the years 1990-2002 with an upward tendency in the years 1994-1997, in which employment never reached the level of the year 1990, the number of workers employed in companies with foreign capital grew steadily. In February 2003, for companies employing more than 10 persons, it was over 968 thousand people, i.e. 22.5% of the total of the companies preparing annual reports[7].

Figure 3: Employment in foreign companies and its share in a total number of companies filing annual reports in the years 1994-2002

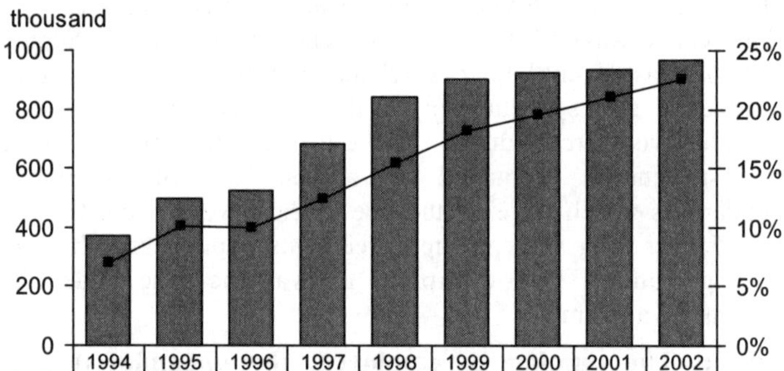

	1994	1995	1996	1997	1998	1999	2000	2001	2002
Employement in thousands	373,9	495,3	525,9	682,8	840,9	901,8	925,8	931,7	968,2
Share	7,0%	10,1%	10,0%	12,5%	15,5%	18,2%	19,6%	21,0%	22,5%

Source: Foreign investment in Poland. Annual report. B.Durka, J.Chojna. IKiCHZ Warszawa 2004, p. 23.

Taking into account micro enterprises one may say that the number may be estimated at 1 million people. The increased rate, which in the years 1997-1998

[7] See Durka /Chojna (2004), pp. 22-26.

was almost 160 thousand decreased annually over the next three years reaching 30 thousand per year. Only in 2002 was this downward trend stopped and significantly greater employment noted than in the two previous years. There was a significant share in employment in the companies with foreign capital operating in financial services (almost 58.6%), in hotel and restaurant business (44.3%), industrial processing (31.6%) and trade and maintenance (28.5%).

Table 3: Employment in companies with foreign capital against the general employment trend in the sector of national industry in 2002, according to industrial categories (as at 31 Dec)

Specifics	Number of employed	Employment in companies with foreign capital against the general unemployment trend according to industrial categories %
Total	4 331 708	X
companies with foreign capital total	968 245	22.5
Incl:		
agriculture, hunting, forestry	4 421	4.6
industry	563 421	26.3
Incl:		
Coal mining, mining	3 355	1.6
Industrial processing	542 563	31.6
Electricity, gas and water	17 503	7.9
Construction industry	22 873	7.8
Trade and maintenance	198 746	28.5
Hotels and restaurants	24 223	44.3
Transportation, warehousing, communication	79 057	16.4
Financial services	18 115	58.6
Real estate and company management	46 652	11.2
Education	591	9.8
Health and social services	2 475	6.4

Source: Foreign investment in Poland, Annual Report. B.Durka, J. Chojna, IKiCHZ, Warszawa 2004, p. 25.

The falling rate of employment was due to poor economic trends, a slumping number of greenfield investments and group redundancies after group work agreements expired.

Generally the share of the global companies within the number of employers in Poland must be considered small for the whole period in question compared with Polish companies. These companies do have a bigger share in profits, however, rather than in employment. In the years 1994-2002 the former rose from 12.4% to 38.1%, while the latter from 7% to 22.5%.

This translated into a much greater work efficiency in foreign-owned companies. Except for the financial services sector it applied to all industrial categories (GDP), reaching the highest level in the transportation sector, as well as in warehousing, and communication – almost 5 times more, and in the construction sector, real estate management - almost three-fold. On average, the efficiency in foreign-owned companies was in the years 1997-2002 two times higher than in Polish companies. This advantage was due to the fact that the former applied newer technologies, better management, and management techniques. Production structure in those companies was modern and it affected the level of the technological advancement in the Polish economy as such. Foreign companies spent more money on raising their staff's qualifications.

Foreign capital investment may be generally divided into three categories from the employment perspective and their influence on employment in Poland. The first category is greenfield, or building a factory or a plant from scratch. This type of investment undoubtedly creates new work places. It accounts for a few dozen percent in the total of investment in Poland. These investments are related mainly to the car industry (Volkswagen in Wałbrzych and Poznań, Toyota in Polkowice and Jelcz Laskowice (dolnośląskie province), Wabco and Volvo in Wrocław, Opel in Gliwice etc.), to the food industry (Danon, Cargil, Nestle, Coca-Cola etc.), and recently also to accounting and IT services, e.g. Hewlett Packard, IBM, Citigroup, Philips, Thompson, Lufthansa, Siemens.

Figure 4: Income from the foreign capital share companies' activities and their share general income of companies filing annual reports in the years 1994-2002

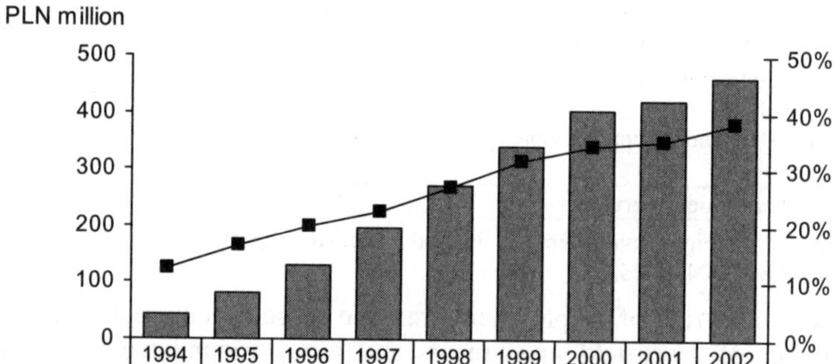

	1994	1995	1996	1997	1998	1999	2000	2001	2002
Income in millions	44,7	79,8	131,5	195,1	270,8	340,9	405,8	420,6	463,0
Share	12,4%	16,6%	20,0%	22,6%	26,8%	31,6%	34,0%	35,1%	38,1%

Source: Foreign investment in Poland, Annual Report. B.Durka, J. Chojna, IKiCHZ, Warszawa 2004, p. 26.

The most important group is related to capital privatization of Polish companies, i.e. transformation of big, state-run companies and the sale of their shares to foreign investors. In fact it was connected in each single case with expiring of group work agreements guaranteeing employment, and resulted in redundancies. One should not draw a conclusion that such activity adversely affected the level of employment in Poland; the shortage of capital would have, in most cases, led to even higher unemployment and bankruptcy in most of these companies.

The third category of FDI is the purchase of a company in order to:

- Eliminate competition and take its share of the Polish market (e.g. production of the medical containers, plant in Bolesławiec which was a monopoly on the Polish market);
- Gaining advantage after selling of the company through the sales of land and premises;
- Taking over its receivables from contractors;
- Using the company in Poland as a loss generating centre; profits generated in other centres abroad (Train Carriers Factory in Ostrowiec);
- Better ways of competition against Polish companies on better economic terms after investing in Special Economic Zones (tax exemption);
- Acquiring a consumer market for its contractors at the expense of the domestic ones (e.g. elimination of Polish suppliers of hops by importing hops concentrate from German suppliers for breweries in Poland). Generally it is estimated that US-$ 1 billion in FDI in Poland results in importing supplies to the tune of US-$ 600 thousand;
- Receiving a state order or a license (Siemens which took over a leading electronics company - Elwro in Wrocław and then closed the company).

5 Future prospects for FDI and its impact on employment

Further inflow of FDI will depend on many factors; both on the world economic trends and assessment of Poland by investors in respect to its attractiveness for investment. So far foreign investors have appreciated the availability of well skilled labour, low labour costs, a big consumer market and well developed network of financial institutions. This in addition to other institutions supporting industry and trade in Poland; they also appreciated a big supply of developed land and premises as well as a big number of companies that can be taken over or purchased. Likewise the good conditions for development of agricultural production (climate and arable land), positive geographic location and general good attitude of the authorities and society towards investors also play a role.

Complicated and ever-changing law, especially tax law, are frequently criticized as is freedom of interpretation of the law by state officers, bureaucracy and corruption, a crippling judiciary system, lack of good roads and highways, traffic jams in cities, high costs of telecommunication, poor co-operation and distribution channels, significant impact of politics on economy, poor entertainment and the lack of schools for foreign children.

On the basis of the rankings prepared by various international institutions it is difficult to conclude how competitive Poland is in terms of FDI. In 2003 according to the A.T. Kearney Agency Poland ranked fourth in terms of investment attractiveness after China, USA and Mexico. According to the Swiss Institute – IMO, in the year 2004, Poland ranked 57th among 60 countries subject to assessment.

It seems, however, that the investment climate in Poland will steadily improve. EU membership guarantees social and economic stability. The free flow of goods, services, capital and labour leads to intensification of such flow. The Polish law and its execution is in line with European standards. Significant aid related to structural and cohesion funds will support the development of education, enterprises and communication infrastructure. The forecasts of economic trends are also positive for the coming years. Economic growth is forecasted is at the level of 5% of GDP annually.

On the other hand, salaries are on the rise and the number of industrial companies that could be privatized is small, which would affect the value of FDI and their relocation to other more attractive countries (Ukraine, Bulgaria, Romania, etc.).

To summarize, it can be assumed that positive factors will dominate and the investment flow will be greater with every year, which will influence employment positively. It must be noted that FDI has an impact on employment in Poland directly, but also indirectly – in the companies that co-operate with domestic ones.

It must be remembered that the promotion of Poland as a country that offers a huge number of well skilled and educated young people, as a country attractive for setting up various types of off-shoring services (accounting, IT, finances, research and development), as well as medical, health and beauty services is also of crucial importance.

Literature

Durka, B. and Chojna, J. (2004): Inwestycje zagraniczne w Polsce. Raport roczny, Warszawa.

Instytut Koniunktur i Cen Handlu Zagranicznego w Warszawie (Economic Trends and Foreign Trade Prices Institute): Annual Reports.

Rymarczyk, J. (2004): Internacjonalizacja i globalizacja przedsiębiorstw, PWE Warszawa.

Sucholiński, A. (2002): Bezrobocie a reastukturyzacja polskiej gospodarki, in: Ekonomia i Międzynarodowe Stosunki Gospodarcze, no. 10, Fiedor, B. and Rymarczyk, J. (eds.) Prace Naukowe AE we Wrocławiu, nr 1007, pp. 38-42.

Warsaw School of Economics (2003): Poland. International Economic Report 2002/2003, Warsaw.

Zorska, A. (2002): Korporacje międzynarodowe w Polsce, in: Difin, pp. 96-103.

The Labour Market in the Polish-German Cross-border Area: Institutional Aspects

by

Franciszek Adamczuk and Andrzej Graczyk

1 Introduction

This paper discusses regional aspects of the labour market. The analysis focuses on the Polish-German cross-border area consisting of three Polish districts Western Pomerania (Zachodnio-Pomorskie), Lubuskie (Area east of the Oder River and Lusatian Neisse) and Lower Silesia (Dolny Śląsk) as well as three German federal states Mecklenburg-Western Pomerania, Brandenburg and Saxony and the capital of the Federal Republic of Germany, Berlin. The access to data and analysis based on the Nomenclature of Territorial Units for Statistics NUTS – 2 of the European Union gave reason to this regional selection. The paper relies on Polish and German research studies of the past years. Furthermore the paper analyses and evaluates unemployment tendencies, which recently occurred in these regions in 2004. In this context it is of major interest, whether unemployment has declined after the access of Poland to the European Union on May 1st 2004. Finally, the paper evaluates and summarizes the main results of the analysis.

2 Institutions designing the labour market

The design of the labour market in a regional and local context is part of the regional policy. It is incumbent upon a variety of institutions:

- Regional self-governing bodies
- Institutions of the business environment
- Employers' associations
- Institutions for statutory accident insurance and prevention (German: Berufsgenossenschaften)

These institutions collaborate with each other and develop certain conditions concerning labour market policy. Especially, they participate in the process of designing the labour market. In the European Union, these questions are controlled by a number of regulations.

Thus, the labour market policy is realized by the following players:[1]

- Employees and their responsible Berufsgenossenschaften,
- Employers (enterprises) and their representations,

---

[1] See Borkowska (2002), p. 323.

- Unemployed and their representations,
- Public hiring agencies, including unemployment insurance
- Other subjects reinforcing the equilibrium on the labour market.

Form and content of the labour market are functions of several factors which result from a country's social-economic policy. In the European Union, the labour market forms a special field of interest of the different bodies. Its evaluation is based on the level of unemployment. Of major interest are the following aspects:

- The mobility between regions,
- Flexibility of employment,
- The educational system,
- Intermediation of vacancies,
- Organisational and legal conditions of the labour market.

The development of the European integration changes the relation to the above mentioned issues in the European Union as a whole as well as in several member countries their self. Generally, all countries are concerned with long term and universal principles relating them to proper interests and needs. Thus the discussion about these points often raises controversial aspects.[2]

3 Characteristics of the labour market in the Polish-German cross-border area

The labour market in the cross-border area is characterized by different attributes.
The most important are:

- Increasing mobility of the workforce, depending on the increased mobility of the population as a whole,
- In-depth knowledge of the labour market (local, regional and international),
- Increased rate in obtaining work experience in the labour market,
- Increased intra working competition,
- Increased meaning of personal, familial and regional relationship for the choice of employment,
- Complexity of factors, that influence somebody's value on the regional labour market, e.g. being unemployed or not.

These are characteristics of the labour market, selected in the Polish and German studies, e.g. in the GÜSA-study for Saxony by E. Steinert. The Polish experts emphasise the differentiation in a regional manner. In doing so, they concentrate on similarities and differences between the Polish and German labour market.

---

[2] See Kabaj (2004).

One example represents the study that was conducted in Poznań and Wrocław. This does in detail the Polish institute for labour and social manners (IPiSS) in Warsaw.[3]

4 Types of cross-border relations on the labour market

The cross-border relations on the labour market in the cross-border area can be grouped as follows:

The first group is composed of typical formal relations. Both sides gain information from each other within the scope of the official standard techniques regarding the characteristics of the labour market e.g. status of employment, structure of employment and education, etc. Those information bases on official statistical sources like statistical offices, organisations of branches or regions and further academic studies. They are available for little or no charge.

The second group is composed of semi formal relations. Those are relations with little extent or content. They emerge sporadically for the solution of similar problems, e.g. improvements in the local labour market, regional preferences.

The third group is composed of non formal relations. They use information with different meaning and credibility. This data is officially written down, derives from hearsay, and is distorted or even not true. The non formal relations are visible by the employment of collaborators: e.g. by the negotiation of hourly wage rates in other regions, and so called minimal norms to get the whole salary et al. These relations are often similarly to mafia relations and could be found mostly in the so called black labour market.

In the Polish-German cross-border area the employees are educated for the demand of both countries. Between 1990 and 2004 70000 Polish employees participated in different training courses in Germany and further EU-countries. Otherwise appr. 1500-2000 non Polish employees were educated in Poland; that includes the period of probation inside the companies with German shareholders. This shows a strong disequilibrium. During this period 600 education programs existed to enrich the cross-border labour market. According to German sources there are appr. 15000 Polish citizens enrolled at a German and appr. 1000 Polish citizens enrolled at a Polish college/university. This shows another disequilibrium. In the Polish-German cross-border area two new universities were built, which educate in 18 branch of studies students from both (and further) countries. These are the European University Viadrina Frankfurt (Oder) and the International Graduate School Zittau (IHI).

These are only few chosen activities for designing the labour market in the cross-border area.

---

[3] See Marek (2000).

The cooperation between German and Polish agencies shows a high efficiency relating to placement of seasonal workers or the engagement of workers in Germany that come on special request of German enterprises. Nevertheless, the described areas remain the only ones in cooperation of the German federal states and Poland apart from vocational education or mixed forms like work and qualification. Thus, there is a high potential regarding to an improvement of cooperation. Formal barriers and different workings of the institutions in Poland and Germany are obviously a bar. Though, those issues will not be part of this paper.

To sum up, it can be said that only a small part of the cross-border relations concerns the labour market. Unfortunately, the solution of regional and local problems of the labour market does not follow the principle of bilateral cooperation. Self-governing bodies in the Polish-German cross-border area point out the necessity of creating a new model of cooperation and of a better transfer of German experiences to the Polish market, e.g. regarding training of unemployed people and preparation for a future workplace.

German experiences might useful for the Polish labour market policy in the following topics:

1. "Pact for labour" decided on initiative of the German Federal government with participation of labour unions and employers' associations,
2. Tax Reform known as Tax Reform 2000,
3. Programme "Direct campaign for reductions of youth unemployment",
4. "Fairs for training", arranged by cities, townships and regions,
5. Programme "Germany 21" for the promotion of the information society
6. Project "Women and internet"

It is self-evident that these selected experiences cannot be taken over to the Polish labour market without appropriate corrections and adaptations to Polish conditions.

5 Efficiency of institutional solutions to promote the labour market in the cross-border area between Germany and Poland

Within a huge number of institutions, which exert vital influence on the formation of economic relations between Poland and Germany, the following ones are particularly to be stated:

Polish-German Society for Promotion of the economy,
Polish-German Chamber of Industry and Commerce

Within the scope of their statutory tasks these institutions deal directly or indirectly with the labour markets in both countries in special consideration of the Polish-German cross-border area.

Among many realized projects of the last years some schemes can be found that forward the common labour market in Poland and Germany, in particular in the cross-border area. This can be considered as an important contribution to the common objectives and both institutions design conditions for cooperation of business units in third country markets. These aspects will not be amplified in this place. The results concerning the consolidation of fixations of the regional and local labour markets between Poland and Germany unfortunately remain insufficient and not-satisfactory. Polish as well as German specialists are pointing out this deficiency.

Analyzing the experiences of institutions that form the labour market regionally and locally the following observations can be made:

- Distinct preferences for local instead of supra-local issues, that leads to an inclusion of townships and cities instead of districts and higher administrative districts,
- Restricted cooperation of administrative agencies establishing conditions for a solution (reduction) of the problems on the labour market,
- Consideration of labour market problems in regional development strategies as a medium for regional development instead of an end in itself,
- Restricted exchange of experience for the purpose of complex problem solution,
- Application of typical standard means on the labour market correspondent to usual EU Directives or in conformity with other directives that are subject to the procedures of financial support by the European funds.

It exist a large number of regional and local development institutions that deal indirectly with labour market problems in the Polish-German cross-border area, among others agencies of regional development, Chambers of Industry and Commerce, business incubator, manufacturers associations, entrepreneur associations, merchants associations, employers' associations and even labour unions. All named institutions participate in the transnational solution of issues concerning the labour market in the border area. Their activities are not explained in this paper.

6 Changes of the state of unemployment in the Polish-German border area

The accedence of Poland to the EU was expected to bring positive changes of the economy and employment. The German side did not open the labour market for the Polish people but the flow of goods and particularly the movement of services between both countries have increased. It might be expected that the movements are activated especially in the border area since German enterprises could take advantage of low cost of labour to invest and produce in this region.

This would reduce the unemployment rate in the Polish-German border area especially in townships and cities closely to the border.

To confirm this hypothesis unemployment data ascertained for districts and counties was statistically analyzed. This data is monthly publicised by the Polish statistical office. In the first instance the changes of unemployment rates in the districts bordering Germany (from north to south: Western Pomerania, Lubuskie and Lower Silesia) were analyzed. In all of the aforementioned districts the unemployment rate exceeded the average rate of Poland. Illustration 1 shows a comparison of the unemployment rates of the three districts and Poland at the end of each month in the year 2004. The decrease of the unemployment rate in Poland and in the analyzed districts already began in February, two month before Poland joined the European Union. In Poland the unemployment has decreased systematically since March similar to the situation in the district of Lubuskie, Lower Silesia and Western Pomerania. In the latter district the fall stopped in August 2004. Thus, it cannot be stated out that the joining of Poland to the EU improved the situation on the Polish labour market.

Figure 1: Unemployment rate in Poland and in the Germany-bordering districts

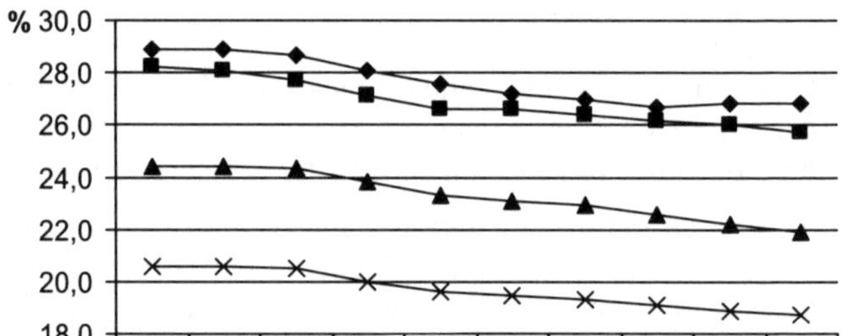

	Jan	Feb	Mar	Apr	Mai	Jun	Jul	Aug	Sep	Oct
ZACHODNIOPOMORSKIE	28,9	28,9	28,7	28,1	27,6	27,2	27,0	26,7	26,8	26,8
LUBUSKIE	28,2	28,1	27,7	27,1	26,6	26,6	26,4	26,2	26,0	25,7
DOLNOŚLĄSKIE	24,4	24,4	24,3	23,8	23,3	23,1	22,9	22,6	22,2	21,9
POLEN	20,6	20,6	20,5	20,0	19,6	19,5	19,3	19,1	18,9	18,7

In table 1 the differences between the unemployment rate of Poland as a whole and the analyzed districts are displayed. It can be seen that in April 2004 the difference virtually did not vary in the district of Lubuskie and Western Pomerania and merely in Lower Silesia a reduction was noted. The letter district has as well a border to Czechia so that it is impossible to say that the reduction of the differences was caused by the German economy and not by the Czech economy.

Table 1: Differences between the monthly publicised unemployment rates in the Germany-bordering districts and the unemployment rates in Poland (%)

	Jan	Feb	Mar	Apr	May	Jun	Jul	Aug	Sep	Oct
Western Pomerania	8.3	8.3	8.2	8.1	8.0	7.7	7.7	7.6	7.9	8.1
Lubuskie	7.6	7.5	7.2	7.1	7.0	7.1	7.1	7.1	7.1	7.0
Lower Silesia	3.8	3.8	3.8	3.8	3.7	3.6	3.6	3.5	3.3	3.2

The analyzed districts are huge administration units counting several million inhabitants. The eastern borders of the districts Western Pomerania and Lower Silesia are over 200 km away from their western borders. The unemployment can be strongly influenced by other factors and the influence by the German economy on the unemployment of the analyzed districts might be weak. For the purpose of analyzing this relation the unemployment rates of counties nearby the border were determined.

Figure 2: Unemployment rate in the year 2004 in the counties closely to the German border situated in the district of Western Pomerania in comparison with the average rate of all districts and Poland as a whole (%)

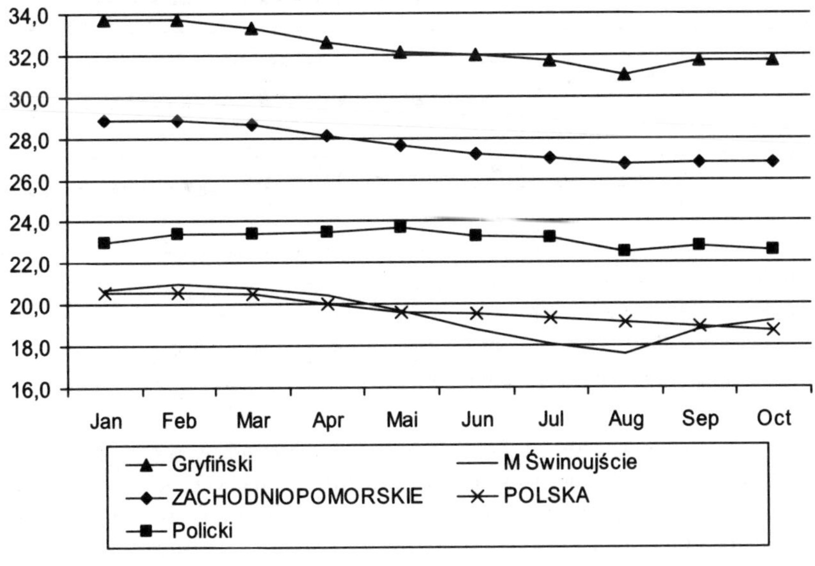

Figure 2 demonstrates the situation in the counties in Western Pomerania. As a comparison the tendencies of the unemployment rates of Poland as a whole and of the district to which the discussed counties belong are shown.

In Figure 2 it is easy to see that merely in Świnoujście (Zwinemünde) the unemployment rate is on a level with the average Polish rate. However, Zwinemünde can be considered as a city with the specific characteristic as a seaport and a health resort. Thereby the decrease of the unemployment rate during holiday time and the increase after September can be explained. In the other counties the decrease of the unemployment rate was more slowly than in the district of Western Pomerania, especially in the county of Gryfino after May 2004.

In figure 3 the situation in the counties of the district of Lubuskie is shown. In the two counties Słubice und Żary (district Lubuskie) the decrease of the unemployment rate after May 2004 is minimal. A similar development can be seen in the county of Krosno in the period from May to August. Only since September a decrease of the unemployment rate is visible.

Figure 3: Unemployment rate in 2004 in the Germany-bordering counties of Lubuskie in comparison with the average rate of all districts and Poland as a whole (%)

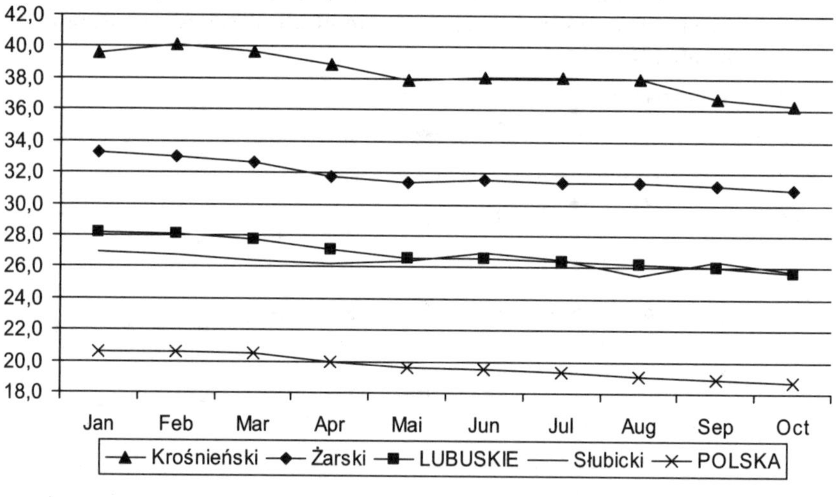

The situation in the county of Zgorzelec is demonstrated by figure 4. Zgorzelec is the unique county in the district of Lower Silesia that verges on Germany. In this county the unemployment rate until April was almost similar to those of the whole district of Lower Silesia. Compared with this, since May the decrease of the unemployment rate was slower in the county of Zgorzelec than in Lower

Silesia. The result is that in the end of October the unemployment rate in Zgorzelec is much higher than the average rate of all districts.

Figure 4: Unemployment rate in 2004 in the Germany-bordering counties of Lower Silesia in comparison with the average rate of all districts and Poland as a whole (%)

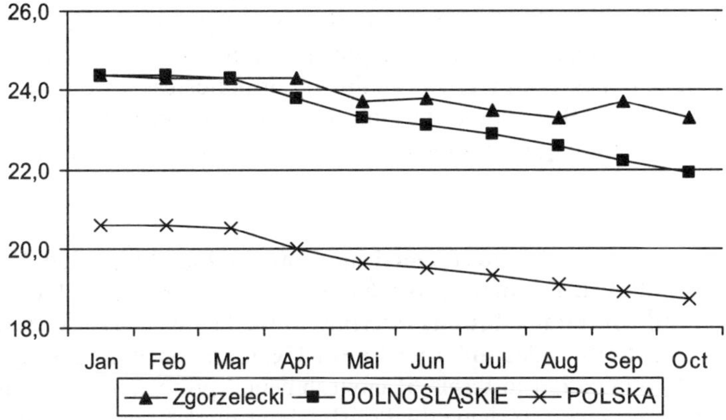

On the basis of the demonstrated tendencies of the unemployment rates it can be reasoned that Poland's integration into the European Union probably did not have an influence on the decrease of the unemployment rate in the Germany-bordering regions. The data of table 2 seems to confirm this statement.

Table 2: Deviation of the average unemployment rate of counties closely to the border from the average rate of the districts to that the county belongs, year 2004 (%)

	Jan	Feb	Mar	Apr	May	Jun	Jul	Aug	Sep	Oct
Zgorzelecki	0.0	-0.1	0.0	0.5	0.4	0.7	0.6	0.7	1.5	1.4
Krośnieński	11.4	12.0	12.0	11.8	11.3	11.5	11.7	11.8	10.7	10.6
Słubicki	-1.3	-1.4	-1.3	-0.9	-0.2	0.3	0.1	-0.7	0.4	0.1
Żarski	5.1	4.9	4.9	4.6	4.8	5.0	5.0	5.2	5.2	5.2
Gryfiński	4.8	4.8	4.6	4.5	4.5	4.8	4.7	4.3	4.9	4.9
Policki	-5.9	-5.5	-5.3	-4.6	-3.9	-3.9	-3.8	-4.2	-4.0	-4.2
Stadt Świnoujście	-8.2	-7.9	-7.9	-7.7	-7.9	-8.4	-8.9	-9.1	-8.0	-7.6

In this table the differences between the monthly unemployment rates of the counties closely to the border and of the districts to which the counties belong to are shown. A positive value implies that the unemployment in the county is higher than in the "Mother-district". If the positive value increases or a negative value displaces towards a positive value the unemployment in the county will rise compared with those of the particular district. This tendency can be noted in almost all counties except in Krosno. This was strengthened after Poland's access to the EU (after April 2004).

This might refer to the insufficient character of purely "market-oriented" activities that aim at the improvement of the employment situation in cross-border areas. The introduction of free movement of goods and services did not have the desired effect on the unemployment rate in the border area because of the restrictions imposed on tourism. Indirectly, it indicates as well the weakness of those institutions that should develop the economic relations. This confirms the necessity of building institutional solutions that improve this situation.

7 Final remarks

As can be seen from the performed analysis during the period 1990 until 2005 in the Polish-German cross-border area there is a lack of self-executing and common solutions referring to the labour market **to reduce the problems on both sides of the Polish-German border** despite several examples of cooperation in terms of environmental protection, development of business initiatives etc. To shape the Polish labour market some European experiences (to a lesser extent German experiences as well) are used.[4] It can be supposed that the high unemployment in the newly-formed German states influences the employment policy of Germany and Poland. The high unemployment in Poland exerts influence on the German policy towards Polish citizens.

Since May 1st of 2004 the amplification of the EU has not caused essential changes on the home labour market, a fact that as well is expressed by the employer's association in Poland. The introduction of a transitional agreement that citizens coming from new EU-countries cannot be staffed in Germany for seven years after the amplification of the respective country (among others: Poland) can be considered as an engraving obstacle to the liberalization of the bilateral Polish-German relations. After having observed the effects of the Polish access to the EU on the labour market the German misgivings seem to be unsubstantiated. Even though, they left negative effects on the labour market in Poland that are weighty and hard to make up for. The introduction of the free movement of goods and services in the year 2004 did not have enough effect on the labour market to compensate the negative effects of the transitional agreement not to staff citizens from Poland The unemployment rate in counties closely to the border did not change in comparison to those in the particular districts.

---

4 See Kryńska (2001), pp. 121-123.

The different treatment of the newly-formed German states and regions in other countries within the EU is to be considered as a dangerous precedent case that will lead to a breach of the mechanism of equality of all countries and regions in the EU, now as well as after further amplifications. This problem can be seen on the labour market, especially in the Polish-German cross-border area.

The regional problems (obstacles to the development) on the labour market inhibit the social prosperity and the improvement of living conditions and quality of citizens, which seems to be an important reason for the further liberalization of the regional and international labour market especially in the EU.

Literature

Adamczuk, F. (2004): Bereiche und Formen der wirtschaftlichen Zusammenarbeit im polnisch-deutschen Grenzgebiet, in: in: Współczesne problemy polityki ekonomicznej (red) Z. Przybyła, J. Sokołowski, prace Naukowe AE nr 1033, Wrocław.

Kabaj, M. (2004): Strategien und Programme der Arbeitslosigkeitsbekämpfung In der EU und in Polen, Warszawa.

Marek, E. (2000): Beschäftigung der Polen im Ausland. Beschäftigung der Ausländer in Polen, Informator, IPiSS Warszawa.

Golinowska, S. (1998): Wirtschaftliche Entwicklung der Regionen. Arbeitsmarkt. Migrationsprozesse, IPiSS Warszawa.

Polnisch-deutsche Gesellschaft für Wirtschaftsförderung AG (2001): Deutscher Markt. Ratgeber für Exporteure und Investoren, Kolonia - Gorzów Wkp.

Borkowska, S. (2002): Arbeitsmarkt und die Integration mit der EU, IPiSS Warszawa.

Kryńska, E. (2001): Anregung der Arbeitskraftbeweglichkeit. Methoden und Instrumente, Raport IPi SS nr 20, IPiSS Warszawa.

Szolek, K. (2004): Trends in der grenzüberschreitenden Zusammenarbeit zwischen Polen und Deutschland, in: Przybyła, Z. and Sokołowski, J. (eds.), Współczesne problemy polityki ekonomicznej, (red), Prace Naukowe AE nr 1033, Wrocław.

The Institutional Aspects of Personal Capital Investments

by

Bożena Klimczak

1 Introduction

The influence of education on the possibility of creating future incomes was first noticed by A. Smith in "Wealth of Nations". This idea was brought back and developed in the 1950s by G. Becker, J. Mincer and T.W. Schultz. They emphasized the importance of education and the role it plays in various economic phenomena, such as work efficiency and the level and disparities of incomes. Later on economists pointed out at the influence education can exert on economic growth.[1] The thesis saying that a higher level of education hastens the growth and development of an economy suggests that the government should carry out a policy of improving educational achievements. Thus, many economists and international organisations claim that educational investments should be a priority for countries trying to cover the development gap and experiencing high levels of unemployment.[2]

The purpose of this paper is to critically and conclusively present the theory from which the above mentioned thesis arises and to examine its empirical status. The theory of human capital will be discussed in the first place, its implications and alternative hypotheses indicating premises other than education for acquiring a labour market entitlement. In the second part of the paper those alternative hypotheses will serve as a starting point for developing the concept of institutional entanglement of individual educational choices and social choices pertaining to investments in education. At last, the critical discussion of human capital theory and the introduction of other forms of personal capital will enable formulation of a hypothesis about the place of education in the social process of training mobile and active participants of the labour market.

2 The role of education in human capital theory

The human capital theory is founded on classical economy intuitions and on the theoretical model of neoclassical economy. A. Smith in "Wealth of Nations" presented some basic relations between spending on acquiring abilities needed for working and incomes received from this work:

1. spending on education brings about higher incomes in the future as it increases work efficiency,

---

1 See Lucas (1988), Barro (1991), Mankiw / Romer / Weil (1992).

2 See Becker (1995), World Bank (2001).

2. spending on teaching and training of professional competences is returned in future incomes,
3. income disparities can be explained by education spending disparities.

These linkages have served as a base for constructing the human capital theory. This capital has basic features of physical capital. Firstly, it is a stock that can be increased with time but also can be used up. Secondly, it is a private stock. These two features mean that human capital is comprised of private knowledge and intellectual and professional abilities. The growth of human capital is the result of a learning process undergoing in educational and training system. The relinquishment of education against the progress of common knowledge leads to the consumption of personal knowledge and qualifications. Access to common knowledge calls for expenditure, which corresponds with the third feature of capital – the rational choice between present expenses and future benefits gained from human capital. The theory of human capital considers then the choice of the level and type of education as a choice between present and future consumption. To give just one example, parents' decision about education of their children, in a simple model, consists in maximising utility U, comprised of: consumption during the education period C_1, increase of consumption in the period when parents discount the benefits of having educated children δC_2, and the satisfaction of having educated offspring δA:

$$U = C_1 + \delta C_2 + \delta A.$$

Parents make therefore the choice about spending for education of their children for the sake of two reasons: the increase in future consumption and the satisfaction from having educated children.[3] Education spending creates human capital A, which depends on the child's abilities α, the quality of school Q, and the time of schooling (S):

$$A = \alpha f(Q)\, g(S).$$

The creation of human capital can be considered then as a private investment in the ability to bring about future incomes, similarly to a physical or financial investment. The fourth feature of human capital is the possibility of transferring the property rights. Human capital as a private stock of knowledge and capabilities can be transferred from one person onto another; in the process of teaching the teacher conveys his knowledge to pupils and shapes their abilities. If this transfer takes the form of an exchange then it is a source of education spending.

Investing in human capital, like all investments, is the result of a rational calculation: if net benefits gained from it are greater than net benefits gained

---

[3] See Gleewe (2002).

from any other investment, than a rational individual chooses education. This implication however was not confirmed during empirical studies, which have emphasized the social costs and benefits of education. Public and private costs and benefits are so much interconnected that it is hardly possible to separate private calculation and private choice. It applies not only to elementary and secondary but also to the higher level of education. The studies of G. Psacharopoulos on private and social rate of return indicated in the first place that both indexes decreased with an increase in the level of education.[4] The lowest growth rates of spending on higher education were observed for countries with highest incomes, where there is a significant supply of highly qualified workers. Secondly, the social rate of return was always higher than the private one. Thus, using a private economic calculation, one can come up with the conclusion that it is better to invest in some other form of resources than education. Yet in countries with obligatory education at some levels, a part of human capital is not a private investment. It is then worth considering an alternative choice: between investment in criminal capital and investment in education, reputation and social contacts.[5] Such methodology can be justified by the results of some studies not confirming the thesis that education and training directly increase work efficiency, and thus bring higher incomes.[6] It has been confirmed at present times and it even served D. Card to formulate the sheepskin hypothesis: higher earnings are rather the consequence of certificates and scientific degrees than qualifications.[7] Without making a bigger mistake one can claim that such relation existed in Poland in 1990s. Spending on higher education was an individual private investment in the ability to create future incomes. It has not been connected though with the creation of human capital, defined as the private stock of knowledge, intellectual abilities and professional competences.

The above cited studies induce to wander off from searching for a positive relation between spending on education and future incomes. It would be essential to establish the effectiveness of education in order to confirm not only this positive relation but also a negative influence of education on potential labour productivity and thus on future incomes. It is worth mentioning that this alternative hypothesis was devised by J.K. Arrow who claimed that education not only gives diplomas but it also works as a filter which establishes abilities

4 See Psacharopoulos (1985).

5 See Hagan / McCarthy (1998).

6 See Blaug (1976).

7 See Card (1999); It is a reference to sociological concept of credentialism.

and dispositions. If schools, especially at the university level, perform such a role, then its effect is to provide the right man with the right job.[8]

The other alternative hypothesis has grown from a critical attitude towards the human capital theory for the sake of lacking an institutional context. In particular, the human capital theory took into consideration neither the capabilities, nor family or closest society upbringing, nor the motivation accompanying the educational investment choices.

Summing up, the role of education in the creation of human capital is significant. However, in the human capital theory it was simplified and by that exaggerated. Attending schools at various level of education might, but does not have to be an investment that is returned from future earnings. Education is necessary but not sufficient. Firstly, there are other tools and ways of increasing future incomes. Secondly, the effect of education may consist in the magic of diplomas. Thirdly, apart from human capital, one needs an additional capital to function actively in the economy.

3 The institutional aspect of human capital investments

The knowledge of the role of education in creating human capital is incomplete. It was quite easy to prove that there is no direct relation between education and efficiency or entrepreneurship. However, there are still too few studies on education effectiveness, on the relation between intellectual qualifications and private and public benefits of education.[9] Such studies are needed to verify the following hypotheses:

- human capital as a stock of private knowledge, abilities and qualifications is a source of legal private incomes provided that it is supplemented by social capital;[10]
- individual choices in education do not consist solely in choosing a particular school and time span of schooling, in the context of resigning from current consumption in favour of future consumption; one can consider as primary or equivalent the choice of investment in criminal capital, understood as the stock of knowledge, abilities, qualifications and bindings useful for committing crimes;[11]
- human capital can be used to attain private benefits from a legal activity consisting in "unproductive entrepreneurial activities".[12]

---

[8] See Arrow (1973).

[9] See Gleewe (2002).

[10] See Coleman (1988).

[11] See Hagan / McCarthy (1998).

[12] See Baumol (1990).

Human capital is considered in these hypotheses as a potential stock,[13] the use of which depends on some additional factors. G. Becker indicated the importance of government's legislative choices[14] and W. Baumol – "the structure of payoffs in the economy – the rules of game"[15]. There is lots of evidence in Poland indicating that human capital is socially misused, although it is obtained in socially promoted educational system. This relates to lawyers, accountants, investment advisers, but also to journalists, politicians and civil servants. Here one is faced with the choice of human capital usage that brings a higher rate of return.

Additionally, the studies of teenage crime suggest that in certain circumstances a choice is made between being educated by the schooling system and training enabling to commit profitable crimes.[16] In a deeper insight into this matter one should take account of positive risks coming not only from the choice of criminal usage of human capital, but also from the lack of information about labour market and unpredictability of the changes in the growth rate and structure of the economy.

In presented hypotheses an economic concept of social capital is used, derived from social sciences[17] and conceptualised by R. Putman and J. Coleman[18]. Their works, as well as works of other scientists from that circle, express a great spirit of civil engagement, effecting in the creation of social networks comprised of different kinds of associations, groups, and communities. Their abundance and quality exert a positive influence on economic growth and development. The hypothesis, called the Putman effect, was placed in opposition to Olson's hypothesis from 1965. Olson claimed that associations and other relations among people who have a common interest in seeking an economic rent have unfavourable influence on economic growth. Putman's hypothesis could be formulated because its author used the notion of "capital" in a non-economic sense. Social capital is not a stock owned by a proprietor who makes conscious choice of relinquishment in favour of future benefits. Social capital is comprised of *characteristic features of social life – network, norms and trust – that facilitate the co-operation and co-ordination for mutual benefit.*[19] Therefore, if financial, physical and human capital is an investment preceding benefits connected

---

[13] See Mincer (1977).
[14] See Becker (1995).
[15] Baumol (1990).
[16] See Leung (2002).
[17] See Tocqueville de (1961).
[18] See Putman (1997), Coleman (1988).
[19] See Putman (1997).

personally with earlier inputs, then social capital contributes functionally to achieving social benefits.

Putman's hypothesis is based on a metaphorical use of the notion of "capital" and on the explanation of economic benefits by means of functions performed by civil society. However, it includes a deep intuition, inducing a serious insight and profound studies. For the sake of the point at issue, one has to pay special attention to the relation between social capital and education. J. Coleman, R. Putman and other scientists of the genre claim that school education is more effective if parents and local society present some degree of civil commitment in the field of education.[20] The growth of education effectiveness is accompanied then by the growth of social capital. Intuitively this hypothesis seems worthwhile. It can be supported by many examples of beneficial actions of local societies, also in Poland. One is nevertheless allowed to say that civil engagement can have a destructive influence on the quality of education when it consists in demanding to teach selected theories, e.g. creationism instead of Darwinism, or in extorting the so called stress less teaching from teachers. This hypothesis can be supported by lots of evidence, too. It becomes clear then, that R. Putman assumed social capital to be socially beneficial. Nonetheless, one cannot reject the possibility that human capital can be destructive or criminal.[21] In order to consider this hypothesis and to formulate it in a way that it becomes testable, social capital has to be defined, in the first place, within the aspect of individual choices, because various forms and essence of civil commitments, their durability or disappearance are the result of conscious decisions. Secondly, private benefits rising from the influence of social environment, which cannot be consciously chosen for the sake of the place and time of one's birth and education, have to be differentiated from private benefits resulting from a conscious choice of education, social groups and institutional environment. Thirdly, it is indispensable to establish, whether and in what way, private benefits become social benefits.

These stipulations ensue from accepting an economic perspective to the studies of social capital.[22] Social capital is therefore a personal stock comprised of the abilities to use institutions, social networks, to participate in groups and to build social image. This stock added to human capital augments the possibilities of a person to receive greater incomes or any other benefits. I call it a personal

---

[20] See Coleman / Hoffer (1987), Braatz / Putman (1996), Francis et al. (1998).

[21] See Portes / Landolt (1996).

[22] The inspiration to an economic expression of human capital comes from Pierre Bourdieu, a French sociologist. See Bourdieu (1986).

capital, as opposed to human capital.[23] Similarly to human capital, social capital can also be used in a socially beneficial or non-beneficial way. In the latter social capital is built upon, for instance, the relinquishment of school education or simulation of it and participation in a criminal group. The possession of criminal human and social capital can become in certain circumstances a source of high incomes with comparatively the same level of risk: penalisation versus unemployment. Apart from having human capital and social capital in the mentioned meaning, a person can have an immeasurable personal capital, consisting of capabilities and inclinations that are innate or acquired in the early childhood. This capital can also be used in a beneficial or non-beneficial way for the society. Indeed it does not emerge as a private and consciously chosen personal investment, but one cannot abstract from it out of at least two reasons. Firstly, it is the foundation on which human and social capital is built. Secondly, it arises, to some extent, from the choices of parents.

Conceptualisation of human capital as private stock bringing benefits for the society might come across some reservations. The reservations pertain to the usage of personal calculation to make a choice of the path through one's life and of the way of exploiting personal knowledge, competences and abilities. It is worth noticing that the presented concept does not cover all the choices made within the social context, but only those that influence the productivity of human resources and thus should be included in economic growth models. Therefore the concept does not cover only the choices emerging from unselfishness, straightforwardness and good feelings. Private cost and benefit calculation concerning personal capital comprises:

1. choices of parents about education of their children (presented above),
2. choices of teenagers about allocating their time for learning at schools, working, criminal actions and leisure time,
3. choices of adults about further education, participation in groups, building social image, etc.,
4. choices of adults about usage of their personal capital.

Apart from pecuniary costs and benefits, one has to take into account also the non-pecuniary costs and benefits and the probability of their occurrence in the future. Outcome of the calculation depends on the pricing of alternative activities, such as: expected incomes from legal work or crime, expenses on various forms of education and social commitment, penalties for crimes and the probability of a crime discovery, and satisfaction or dissatisfaction coupled with various forms of activity. The level of pricing is directly influenced by present

[23] This concept is similar to concept of storch's „inner goods": social competences. However, it is differut since social competences are the output of social capital relations. See Schumann (2005).

and expected state of economy; indirectly it depends on institutions which set the non-pecuniary costs (penalties) and benefits (rewards) connected with alternative forms of activity and participation. Hence, these institutions can be legal, but also civil, family and criminal. Excluding the latter, all have been incorporated into the broad meaning of social capital, used by R. Putman and J. Coleman; that certainly makes it difficult to separate causes and effects. Yet in an economic concept of personal capital, both human and social, the spectre of institutions is broader and explicitly expressed as an independent variable in individual choice models. It allows for empirical verification of various hypotheses concerning these choices. The purpose of this paper calls for a formulation of a hypothesis about the influence of quality of educational institutions on the choice of investment in human and social capital, which is not only privately, but also socially beneficial.

Educational institutions should be considered at several levels.[24] At the level of state educational institutions are comprised of legal rules, from constitutional to specific ones, setting out duties for the educational system and also rights for the community of teachers. A general framework is created at this level, within which educational activity is to co-operate with parents and pupils and to compete with criminal activities. The convergence of private investment in human and social capital with social expectations is the greater the more intense is the co-operation with families and pupils. Co-operation establishes competition with an explicit criminal activity or with future choice of a socially non-beneficial activity. Thus hypothesis no. 1 emerges: legal framework of educational system serves the purpose of generally directing the choices of investment in human and social capital; yet it does not guarantee the expected private and social benefits in the future.

At the school level institutions are comprised of formal regulations, typical for an organisation and of informal rules and patterns specific for particular schools. Expression and implementation of these institutions, revealed in rigorousness or permissiveness, ascendancy or partnership, and etiquette, shape the culture of a given school. It suggests hypothesis no. 2: the choice of a school for the sake of its culture, determines to a high degree one's personal capital, especially the social capital, and the way it is going to be used.

At the level of teachers, institutions are comprised of professional rules establishing requirements for knowledge and abilities of teachers, and of ethical rules relating to the required moral level of teachers. The worth of these institutions is decisive during the professional selection process and it affects the quality of education and endowment in social capital. This suggests hypothesis

---

[24] The notion of an institution is used in a way it is understood by new institutional economics. See North (1984).

no. 3: private and social benefits arising from educational institutions are to the highest extent dependent on the institution of a teacher's profession.

To verify these hypotheses one can use methods of comparative analysis of schools, professional and income careers of its alumni, and methods of studying influence of various institutions (not only educational) on the choice of the path through life made by pupils and their incomes. The latter were conducted in immigrant communities in the USA and provided valuable information about the fact, that formal education brings lower incomes than education enriched in social capital.[25] Perfecting educational institutions serves then the productivity growth of personal capital.

4 Conclusions

In this paper I analysed economic theory of human capital and sociological theory of social capital in order to establish the role of education in building both kinds of capital. After revealing the hidden assumptions of both theories, a concept of personal capital was formulated – the capital consisting of human and social capital. It allowed for emphasizing private choices connected with investments in this kind of capital and for formulating hypotheses concerning the influence of various educational institutions on pricing of alternative possibilities to invest in personal capital. Studies conducted in many countries support these hypotheses. It means that productivity growth of personal capital depends on perfecting the educational institutions. In a stipulatory approach, it is a suggestion to invest in educational system in twofold meaning: to invest in human capital and in social capital of the teachers.

Literature

Arrow, J.K. (1973): Higher Education as a Filter, in: Journal of Public Economics, no. 2.

Barro, R. (1991): Economic Growth in a Cross-Section of Countries, in: Quarterly Journal of Economics, no. 2.

Baumol, W.J. (1990): Entrepreneurship: Productive, Unproductive and Destructive, in: Journal of Political Economy, vol. 98.

Becker, G. (1995): Human Capital and Poverty Alleviation, in: World Bank Work Paper, no. 52.

Blaug, M. (1976): The Empirical Status of Human Capital Theory, in: Journal of Economic Literature, no.14.

Bourdieu, P. (1986): Forms of Capital, in: Richardson, J.G. (rd.) Handbook of Theory and Research for the Sociology of Education, Greenwood Press, Westport.

---

[25] See Gleewe (2002).

Braatz, J. and Putman, R. (1996): Families, Communities and Education in America: Exploring the Evidence, WCER, Madison.

Card, D. (1999): The Casual Effect of Education and Earnings, in: Handbook of Labour Economics, vol. 31, North-Holland, Amsterdam.

Coleman, J. and Hoffer, T. (1987): Public and Private High Schools: The Impact of Communities, Basic Books, New York.

Coleman, J.S. (1988): Social Capital in the Creation of Human Capital, in: American Journal of Sociology, no. 94.

Francis, P. et al. (1998): Hard Lessons: Primary Schools, Community and Social Capital in Nigeria, in: World Bank Paper, no. 420.

Gleewe, P. (2002): Schools and Skills In Developing Countries: Education Policies and Socioeconomic Outcomes, in: Journal of Economic Literature, vol. XL.

Hagan, J. and McCarthy, B. (1998): Mean Streets: Youth Crime and Homelessness, Cambridge University Press, Cambridge.

Leung, A. (2002): Delinquency, Social Institutions and Capital Accumulation, in: Journal of Institutional and Theoretical Economics, no.158.

Lucas, R. (1988): On the Mechanics of Economic Development, in: Journal of Monetary Economics, no. 22.

Mankiw, N.G., Romer, R. and Weil, D. (1992): A contribution to the Empires of Economic Growth, in: Quarterly Journal of Economics, no. 2.

Mincer, J. (1977): Schooling, Experience and Earnings, New York: NBER.

North, D.C. (1984): Transformation Cost, Institutions and Economic History, in: Journal of Institutional and Theoretical Economics, no. 140.

Portes, A. and Landolt, P. (1996): The Downside of Social Capital, in: The American Prospect, no. 26.

Psacharopoulos, G. (1985): Returns to Education: a Further International Update and Implications, in: Journal of Human Resources, no. 20.

Putman, R. (1997): Democracy in America at Century's End, in: Hadenius, A. (ed.), Democracy's Victory and Crisis, Cambridge University Press, New York.

Putman, R. (1993): Making Democracy Work, Princeton University Press, Princeton.

Schumann, J. (2005): Migration in the Context of Countrie's Human Capital and Social Capital, in: Jahrbuch für Wirtschaftswissenschaften, Vol. 55, No. 1.

Tocqueville de, A. (1961): Democracy in America, Schocken Books, New York.

World Bank (2001): Attacking Poverty, World Development Report 2000/2001, Washington 2001.

Uncertainty and Risk in Perfectly Flexible Labour Market

by

Bogusław Fiedor and Andrzej Matysiak

1 Introduction

The foundation of this article is based on a view which is widely accepted in the main stream economic theory and policy that rigid and inflexible labour market is a source of many negative socio-economic phenomena. There is little doubt that forced unemployment is caused primarily by sticky wages which induce quantitative changes in the labour market. To be precise, the rigid wages themselves do not clear the market, meaning that mutually favourable contracts between the parties are not finalized. The hysteresis theory, on the other hand, clarifies the reasons why rigid labour market fosters persistence of unemployment rates (chronic unemployment). Moreover, the New Keynesian Economics explicates allocative inefficiency of the labour market. Sticky wages and labour social rights significantly reduce the labour cost reduction potential.

The insider–outsider theory alternatively falsifies the common assumption that highly qualified staff has competitive advantage over less qualified workforce. The above view is valid only for the perfectly elastic labour market.[1] We assume that the main cause of the rigidity within the labour market is the impact of legal institutions which exceedingly protect the economic and social interests of the employees. In consequence, those legal provisions seriously limit the employment of:

- long-term unemployed
- women who are willing to work on non-standard terms of employment which are rendered unacceptable by the existing legal framework
- persons who due to age, status or social role would take on jobs based on non-standard terms of employment.

In the light of these assumptions it seems reasonable to postulate deregulation of the labour market, since only the flexible market is able to provide companies with competitive edge within the global economy. Such approach would also prove advantageous for certain social groups, primarily the unemployed women and young people. Another advantage is the fact that promotion and safeguarding of competitive edge of companies brings forth significant gains for all employed, since it also safeguards the existing jobs.

---

[1] There is a huge literature on all of these theories. For a comprehensive surveys and synthesis see, among other things: Bean (1994); Bosworth / Dawkins / Stromback (1996); Lindbeck (1993); Sinclair (1987). A most comprehensive survey in the Polish economic literature has been carried out by Kwiatkowski (2002).

One important question remains: does the deregulation by itself provide sufficient power to establish elastic labour market? This doubt is brought forth by the hypothesis postulating that the elastic labour market generates considerable increase of risk and uncertainty among the employers. In other words, market deregulation positively influences freedom and business potential of the company on elastic labour market at the cost of rising risk and uncertainty. Notably, risk and uncertainty on elastic labour market have a greater effect on the employees than the employers.

The above argument is not conclusive in the dispute over the extent and rate of deregulation measures, since one has to agree that the risk and uncertainty increase tendency is of a more universal nature. "We neither state that the industrial society phase was less risky nor that the risk society has replaced the industrial society. There is, however, a notable distortion between calculable risk on one hand and risk awareness on the other [...]. The global risk society, on all its levels, dutifully feigns control over everything that cannot be controlled, from politics, law, science and economy to everyday life."[2] Hence both the risk generation and the risk negligence stem principally from the unilateral, scientific rationality reduced to economic calculus and absorbed with productivity advantages.[3]

Equally unilateral in its actions is also the market system of contemporary societies, due to the continuing departure or withdrawal of labour unions from the political scene. Without the union force, the labour market tends to favour systems that serve the interest of the employer. We claim that the elastic labour market is an attempt at restructuring the whole society into the market society, in which the division between family life and money earning is slowly fading. Life of whole families and their respective members is subordinated to the employers' requirements. "Each one has to be self-sufficient and subservient to market requirements, to provide for his or her economic subsistence [...]. The fully matured market society is a society without children or with children brought up by highly mobile fathers and mothers".[4]

While the fulfilment of such a dark vision is unlikely, the hypothesis that the elastic labour market significantly endangers the family and child upbringing seems quite plausible. If such a danger is indeed present, one has to seriously consider the scope and range of deregulation. In particular, deregulation may be introduced only when accompanied by certain regulations to protect and absorb the imminent dangers to the family life. Other values jeopardised by the introduction of elastic labour market are outside the scope of this article. Hypotheti-

---

[2] Beck (2002).

[3] See Beck (2002), p. 78.

[4] Beck (2002), pp. 178-179.

cally speaking, the elastic labour market may also prove perilous to the employers, so certain institutions to absorb the shock on that market may be advisable as well. In the light of the above reasoning, the fate of family and child upbringing is put to danger, posing serious threat to the society at large, since the family as an environment to bring up and socialize the young generation is by far indispensable. This is not the only threat posed by introduction of elastic labour market. The risk and uncertainty of employees on elastic labour market is wide-ranging due to position and role of the workers within the national economy. The main factor to discriminate (categorize) the work force on elastic labour market is the human capital value. It seems that the labour market in the years to come will comprise two large groups, mainly:

- knowledge providers, and
- work providers.

The first category of employees will gradually supersede work, thus only in such context one may bring forth such ideas as "the end of work" or "world after work" (Ryfkin). The knowledge providers will, however, be also varied to a certain degree, based on the human capital value they present.

2 Knowledge sector and work

In the history of societies so far, knowledge in general increased work productivity, and its impact on economy manifested in introduction of more efficient and safer machinery, devices and technologies. The progress of knowledge in result led to increase of social productivity as well as changes in labour structure within sectors (agriculture, industry, and services) and overall structural changes that expanded the share of blue- and white-collar work in productive human endeavours. The new sector of science and technology – according to Ryfkin – is a danger to work, as its employment will be marginal "[...] compared to the number of people rendered unemployed by the new generation of 'thinking machines'."[5]

The murky image of "the end of work" stems – as it seems – from failure to recognize development trends within the knowledge sector. In the recent past the sector of knowledge had a public character, meaning that its achievements were made public mainly through education and publication. Parallel to that, the new private sector emerged, developing knowledge in the form of private goods. Privately owned knowledge gradually forms a strategic factor in production, as

---

5 Ryfkin (2001), p. 56. One may be tempted, by contrast, to point analogy to the views of Ricardo, who claims that the workforce dislodged by more efficient and more productive machinery and technologies will find employment in the sector producing such machinery and technologies (the so-called compensation theory of Ricardo).

it determines the position and the competitive advantage of the company. This has been clearly and accurately voiced by P. F. Drucker: "The traditional production factors – the earth (i.e. its natural resources), the work and the capital – have not declined. They became secondary; they can be obtained without difficulties, if one has knowledge. And knowledge in the new meaning of the term has become usability, a means to achieve social and economic results."[6]

Public knowledge is also inadequate for the consumer and the household. It is neither sufficient to fulfil personal curiosity, nor adequate to pursue instrumental aims. Individual demand for knowledge is fuelled by new consumer products, utilization of which requires certain amount of knowledge as to their properties and potential use. Strictly speaking, in the contemporary world knowledge is complementary to the majority of material goods. A good illustration of this is the growing interest in healthy living, proper diet, hygiene and life in the society. Work and life in global environment are considerably dependent on private knowledge, since public knowledge is too general. One may in this context say that knowledge demand is a chance for labour market, and not – as Ryfkin claims – its doom.

Knowledge sector development is dependent on may various factors, the most important of which being, in this case, the level of economic growth, since it may be speculated that knowledge demand is correlated with the amount of GDP per capita. The growth of this sector may, however, be accelerated through institutional chances, notably the introduction of market-oriented knowledge. Such process has already started in respect to knowledge that may be separated from its author (through parents, copyrights, licensing and advisory services). Legal protection of individual knowledge property rights forms provides institutional framework for development of knowledge market open for providers of both small (self-employment) and large enterprises.

Every company needs knowledge of the type that F. A. Hayek describes as "[…] knowledge of precise circumstances of a given time and place."[7] Unfortunately, this kind of knowledge cannot be separated from its creators – namely the human capital. This is also the reason why creation and usage of knowledge in the field of economic processes is still comparable to labour relations. As a matter of fact, this is a process of acquiring knowledge by human capital as a group which through their abilities is able to find knowledge of the type spoken of by F. A. Hayek. To sum up, it may be stated that knowledge created by human capital forms a strategic capital of a company. Fitting its function, this knowledge may be subdivided into knowledge of an organizational, market, technological or other type.

---

[6] Drucker (1999), p. 40.

[7] Hayek (1998), p. 92.

3 Aims and dangers of deregulation on elastic labour market

Let us assume that elastic labour market is functional in respect to the needs of employers and employees, though its operation brings forth an increase in risk for all actors of that market. The distribution of benefits from the introduction of elastic labour market depend on the scale of deregulation and liberalization. These processes are determined by aims we try to achieve by introducing elastic labour market. The respective benefits for the employer may be summed up as:

1. liberating the strategy of employment and shaping it according to employers' preferences
2. adjusting the employment rate and work times to technological and economic parameters of the production process
3. minimizing the cost of hires and lay-offs
4. minimizing the non-wages costs owed to employees and the state
5. optimising the productivity to work cost ratio

The employee profits resulting from maintaining the elastic labour market are:

1. potential for finding a job most suited to employee's individual preferences, such as: work times, place, form of employment contract (clearly defined, for hire, etc.)
2. minimizing the off-work period (between the jobs), since elastic labour market shortens both hire and lay-off time
3. potential to adjust work schedule with other duties (family, training and education, complementary employment)
4. increasing the employment chances for low-qualified staff, due to absence of minimum wages requirement
5. increasing the employment chances for high-risk employees, due to minimal cost of lay-offs and job-hunting.

Based on these presumptions, one may formulate the conclusion that elastic labour market minimizes the cost of adjusting work supply with work demand on both the quantitative and structural level, thus leading to an increase of profits for the employers and the employees. On global scale, the elastic labour market reduces the unemployment rate and social cost thereof. On the other hand, the elastic labour market brings forth certain dangers, most of which are, unfortunately, faced by the employee. This is attributable to the fact that the concepts of elastic labour market wordlessly assume the structural changes to be taking place at the employee end of the scale. It is presumed that work supply should adjust to qualitative and quantitative changes of work demand, since those factors are of more objective nature. To be precise, the technological parameters of production and work should be considered as data, since they are a sign of social and economic development. One may also stress that the employees have to adjust to competitive conditions, and as a result they have to accept the economic parameters of the company, such as the drive to increase productivity and profits as well as the urge to minimize non-wages costs.

It is obvious that in a balanced environment the sum of preferences of both employers and employees has to be harmonized. In this respect, the elastic labour market has to be perceived as profitable for all actors, if it aims to achieve such balance. This ideal situation might as well be neglected, since it is by nature prosaic and free of any problems. Let us, however, try to face the question of problems that the employees may face as a result of elastic labour market introduction. Those problems cannot be avoided, since elastic labour market may operate only when the quantity of rigorous legal provisions is kept at a minimum.

As mentioned above, the main reasons for rigid labour market are:

- legal provisions that regulate minimum wages levels
- legal provisions that specify conditions of employment with regard to work times, lay-off procedures, full-pay leaves, etc.
- legal provisions that impose on the employer certain duties, such as obligatory non-wages charges to the benefit of the employee or the state treasure.

One significant factor to add to rigidity of the labour market is the notion of centralized agreements with trade unions. Decline of unionism or decentralization of group agreements by carrying them over to the company level will certainly boost the labour market elasticity.

It must be stressed, though, that deregulation of labour market through limitation or purging of the aforementioned regulations will lead to a fundamental change in the form of non-standardizing of the work times and workplace. This, in consequence will result in gradual fogging of the boundary between work and leisure.[8] The employment system based on changing, pluralist forms of part-time jobs will – as Ulrich Beck prognoses – be free of unemployment problems, but such an "achievement" will be brought about at the cost of a commonly occurring uncertainty of employment. "Unemployment dies out, but

---

[8] One may find here certain parallels to the leisure class category of T. Veblen. The negative evaluation of this class was based on the fact that the group in question did not in any way contribute to the overall prosperity growth (idle class). On the other hand, the hazards associated with emergence of the non-leisure class (e.g. highly paid managers or freelancers) may be two-fold. Firstly, they take the form of the aforementioned dangers to the family and child upbringing. Secondly, they take on the par excellence economic character, as the long and non-limited work schedule of the non-leisure class imposes certain time limitations for consumption of goods and services. In this respect, while the Veblen's leisure class, despite its idleness, affected the demand and consumption levels, the impact of contemporary non-leisure class on demand and consumption will be far less pronounced when compared with the financial wealth left at their disposal.

appears at the same time and is generalized in new risks of part-time employment."[9]

Without predicting the accuracy of the above prognosis, it must be stated that the existing methods of identification and protection of the unemployed are rendered inadequate in the situation of the elastic labour market. If so, then the new employment system requires simultaneous reform of all institutions that cater for the unemployment issues.

We claim that efficiency of the elastic labour market in addressing the unemployment problem is significantly dependent upon:

- elasticity of wages,
- reduction of non-wages costs, i.e. social benefits and taxes.

A good evidence of the thesis can be found in the effects of the German *geringfügige Beschäftigunsgsverhältnisse* (literally: insignificant/trivial employment), later dubbed Mini Jobs. This scheme was devised to support part-time employment through exemption from income tax and social security payments. By 1999, the employer was obliged to return a lump tax of 22% of the employee's wages. Following the March 24, 1999 regulation, the lump tax was replaced by 10% health insurance instalment plus 22% pension scheme payment out of every part-time job wages. The regulation rendered this type of employment unattractive, since it could not be used as a means of cost reduction.[10]

Mini Jobs have been re-regulated in 2002. The regulation addresses low-paid jobs (up to 800 EUR per month), with no long-term employment contract and no dismissal protection. The jobs are devised for low-qualified staff and people in adverse life situations. They are not covered by trade union schemes. The regulations, in force since April, 2003, state that any employment paid for under 400 EUR is exempt from income tax and social security dues. The employer has to pay 25% lump sum tax for social security. In the case of household Mini Jobs, the income is taxed at 2%, while the social benefit payments are held at 5% for health insurance and 5% for pension scheme payments, respectively. With short-time employment covering periods of no more than 2 months or 50 days per calendar year, the income is altogether exempt from tax and social security payments. German Institute for Economic Research (DIW) reports that in the year 2003 the number of registered Mini Jobs amounted to 7.2 million, with corresponding decrease of standard work agreements.[11]

Questionable as this may be, we tend to regard the Mini Jobs development as a successful example of a labour market reform, although at the price of augmenting the risk and uncertainty of the employees on the labour market. On

---

[9] Beck (2002), p. 212.

[10] See DIW (1998), pp. 873-877.

[11] See Stiftung Marktwirtschaft (2003), p. 3.

the other hand, we believe that decrease of revenues from tax and social security payments is an adequate price for reducing grey market, while lower wages are certainly more appropriate than unemployment benefits. To put it in more general way, fractional wages are a chance of improving the standard of living.

4 Elastic labour market and social imbalance

As stated before, an important result of knowledge sector development and elastic labour market is the segmentation of the labour market. Strictly speaking the segmenting of labour market into free (outside labour market) and institutionalised (in-house labour market) market is based to a large degree on the knowledge criterion. On the outside market all transactions relate to work, while in-house market concerns knowledge incorporated in human capital. The division principles on the two markets are entirely different, since remuneration – or to put it strictly – profit depends here on extent and quality of human capital. The division is meritocratic in character, since the profit is determined by 'merit', or level and quality of education. The employees who offer the highest level of knowledge receive profits based on overall economic performance of the company. Consequently, the conditions may be deemed as propitious for shaping great material imbalance that jeopardize the cohesion of society. The 'winner takes it all' principle results in great polarization of the society, demonstrating in lack of middle group (groups) within its hierarchical structure.

This tendency of elastic labour market to generate serious material disparities has been empirically substantiated. Commenting on the empirical data, M. Carnoy states: "[…] less elasticity on such markets as the German one may lead to an increase in wages and efficiency and a decrease of disparity among those who have jobs, but at the same time a marked rise of unemployment rates, while high elasticity as seen on the US labour market may result in low rise or a decrease of wages and high disproportion of income. This may also suggest that labour markets could be made more elastic at relatively low unemployment rates, high rise of wages and large disproportions between the lowest and highest wages – as is the case of Great Britain – as well as at relatively low rise of wages and insubstantial disproportion of wages – such as is the case of Holland, or at relatively high rise of wages and low disproportion of wages increase – such as in Japan."[12]

To sum up, the US labour market is the closest to the model of elastic labour market and its effects are conclusive in measuring its impact. Among the most important effects of that market (for the period between mid 70s and mid 90s) are:

---

[12] Carnoy (2000), p. 112.

- marked and steady decrease of real wages of most workforce groups, especially with up to the secondary education level, most notably men,
- considerable increase of wages disproportions between employees with university education and those with secondary school education,
- growing disparity in income distribution, in line with the division based on education level, sex, sector of economy and profession.[13]

The elastic labour market is a chance of sorts to meet the principle of equality of sexes, since women are more likely to take on jobs with contracts tailored to individual needs. This may also lead to the fall of cast system with its predominant trait of division of roles and duties based on sex.[14] At the same time, unfortunately, the elastic labour market poses a threat to the family. "Individual competition and mobility called for in the production sphere meet conflicting requirements on family level, such as sacrificing oneself to others and total subordination to collective aims of the family."[15] Maximization of income on elastic labour market and full-time availability required by the employer are hard to reconcile with child upbringing and cultivating family life. In the light of the latter, it seems reasonable to speculate that the in the long run the elastic labour market will lead to drastic birth-rate plunge and rise of youth unfit to live in the society, assuming that child upbringing apart from the family proves ineffective. Painting further this black scheme, one may even venture to suggest that in the historic perspective the fully elastic labour market might lead – through total submission to productivity maximization – to a fundamental undermining of principles of the Western civilization.

State support for the family in the form of modern pre-school and school institutions cannot be perceived as a solution for the problem at hand. This is more of a rerun of the political utopias of the Enlightenment era, an evocation to the state as an idealized and favoured hero of the open-minded and candid liberals. On the other hand, privatisation of upbringing and education as a means of solving discrepancies between the elastic labour market and the need to preserve the traditional family model is an offer addressed only to those few wealthy individuals who can afford to pay for such a far-from-ideal and highly controversial scheme. The only feasible solution seems to be the legal regulation of the so-called availability to the employer, coupled as may be with regulation of maximum work time per day. Appropriate work-time norms apply to industrial machines and devices, and a human being is a far more delicate device than any and all machines and technologies of his creation. That is why, in line

[13] See Carnoy (2000), p. 111.
[14] See Beck (2002), p. 167.
[15] Beck (2002), p. 166.

with the evolution of the species called *homo sapiens*, he should find ample time to rest from work, lest he slowly became nothing more than *homo labourens*.

Contrary to common belief, the elastic labour market poses also certain dangers for the employer. Uncertainty of employment time will decidedly work against such values as the commitment and employee loyalty. The average employee will most likely resume the role of a hireling drawn by the urge to *have* and not to *be*.

Literature

Bean, Ch. R. (1994): European unemployment: A Survey, in: Journal of Economic Literature, vol. 32, pp. 573-619.

Beck, U. (2002): Społeczeństwo ryzyka. [Risk Society] Wydawnictwo Naukowe Scholar, Warszawa 2002.

Bosworth, D., Dawkins, P. and Stromback, T. (1996): The Economics of the Labour Market, Longman, Harlow, Essex.

Carnoy, M. (2000): Sustaining the New Economy. Russell Sage Foundation New York – London.

DIW (1998): Die Reform der 620-Mark-Jobs: Stückwerk, in: DIW Wochenbericht, no. 49, pp. 873-877.

Drucker, P. F. (1999): Społeczeństwo postkapitalistyczne, [Postcapitalist Society] PWN, Warszawa.

Hayek, F. A. (1998): Indywidualizm i porządek ekonomiczny, [Individualism and the economic order] Kraków.

Kwiatkowski, E. (2002): Bezrobocie – podstawy teoretyczne (Unemployment – theoretical foundations), Wydawnictwo PWN, Warsaw.

Lindbeck, A. (1993): Unemployment and Macroeconomics, MIT Press, London.

Ryfkin, J. (2001): Koniec Pracy, [The End of Work] Wydawnictwo Dolnośląskie, Wrocław.

Sinclair, P. J. (1987): Unemployment; economic Theory and Evidence, Blackwell, Oxford.

Stiftung Marktwirtschaft (2003): Im Schneckentempo Richtung Zukunft Deutschland. Ein Jahr nach der Wahl, Berlin.

Internationale Marktwirtschaft

Herausgegeben von Gustav Dieckheuer,
Karl-Hans Hartwig und Theresia Theurl

Band 1 Gustav Dieckheuer / Bogusław Fiedor (eds.): Aspects of Sustainable Economic Development. 2000.

Band 2 Monika Markmann: Entstehung und Beharrungstendenz des "Informellen Sektors". Eine kritische Analyse bisheriger Erklärungsansätze aus institutionenökonomischer Sicht. 2001.

Band 3 Gustav Dieckheuer / Bogusław Fiedor (eds.): Competition, Environment and Trade in the Globalized Economy. 2002.

Band 4 Gustav Dieckheuer / Bogusław Fiedor (eds.): Eastward Enlargement of the European Union. Economic Aspects. 2003.

Band 5 Hannes Ischia: Zentralisierung und Subsidiarität. Eine politökonomische Analyse dieses Spannungsfeldes in der Europäischen Union. 2004.

Band 6 Gustav Dieckheuer / Bogusław Fiedor (eds.): Employment Issues in the European Union. 2006.

www.peterlang.de

Peter Lang · Europäischer Verlag der Wissenschaften

Hartmut Hirsch-Kreinsen / David Jacobson /
Staffan Laestadius (eds.)

Low-tech Innovation in the Knowledge Economy

Frankfurt am Main, Berlin, Bern, Bruxelles, New York, Oxford, Wien, 2005.
334 pp., num. graf.
ISBN 3-631-53682-8 / US-ISBN 0-8204-7700-1 · pb. € 56.50*

This volume brings together reflections and research findings on so-called low-tech industries. The accepted wisdom seems to accept that mature, industrialised nations are undergoing a fundamental transformation into the much vaunted Knowledge Society. There is a firm belief that in this situation the advancement of high-tech industries is essential for growth and development. Correspondingly, in this scenario so-called low-tech sectors appear to be less important in and for the major industrialised countries. The starting point of this volume is a fundamental critique of this widely held belief. In fact, many of the processes we witness today are based on developments outside the realm of high-tech and low-tech industries are important not only for employment and growth but also for knowledge formation in European economies.

Contents: Issue presented in broad overview · Conceptual and definitional questions dealing with knowledge firmation and innovation · Preliminary empirical findings from different industries and sectors · Conclusion: consideration of some of the implications of low-tech research for policy

Frankfurt am Main · Berlin · Bern · Bruxelles · New York · Oxford · Wien
Distribution: Verlag Peter Lang AG
Moosstr. 1, CH-2542 Pieterlen
Telefax 00 41 (0) 32 / 376 17 27

*The €-price includes German tax rate
Prices are subject to change without notice

Homepage http://www.peterlang.de